I HEAR HIS

Whisper

FOR WOMEN

365 Daily Meditations & Declarations

BroadStreet
PUBLISHING

BroadStreet Publishing® Group, LLC
Savage, Minnesota, USA
BroadStreetPublishing.com

I HEAR HIS *Whisper* FOR WOMEN

365 Daily Meditations & Declarations

978-1-4245-6159-9 (faux leather)
978-1-4245-6160-5 (e-book)

Stock or custom editions of BroadStreet Publishing titles may be purchased in bulk for educational, business, ministry, fundraising, or sales promotional use. For information, please email orders@broadstreetpublishing.com.

Cover and interior by Garborg Design at GarborgDesign.com

Printed in China

21 22 23 24 25 5 4 3 2 1

Dedication

Dedicated to two amazing women who sparkle with life
and whose laughter warms my soul.

My daughters, Charity Ann and Bethany Joy.
Special, unique, and sweet.

I cherish you both as God's gift to me.

Introduction

What does it mean to be a woman made in the image of God? It means you can carry him, reflect him, and embrace him as your friend. God, the Creator of every heart, created you to love, to nurture, and to embrace. Each day's whispers are meant to soothe and encourage your heart. The deepest place within you is capable of hearing and responding to the words contained within these pages. They are written for you, God's precious, captivating daughter.

As you bring your heart before heaven each day, you'll receive a message meant to set you on a path of discovery—a delightful discovery of how God sees you. You may be surprised when you hear of this love that gives everything away and spares nothing. The love of Jesus fills each page. Let the whispers from the heart of God quench your thirst and carry you through your days. Enjoy!

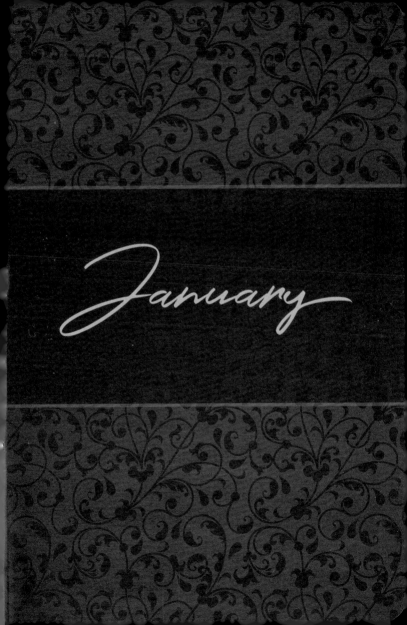

January

Hold to the vision.

A s time passes, I remain the same. I am constant in love, steadfast in truth, and loyal in pursuit. Nothing can alter my character—no situation can affect my compassion. I will transform every hardship with the flood of my love. Remember what I spoke to you in the beginning when you first heard my voice. My promises are true, and I will never let you down.

Have the winds of change confused your senses? Lean into my love today, and you will find that the plumb line of my mercy will make everything come into alignment once again. Though seasons shift and unknowns are inevitable, nothing is a mystery to me. Realign your heart with mine. Let trust be the rhythm that centers you through your every breath. When your mind is flooded with information that distracts, come back to the foundation of your very being. I am the God who created you, and I have not wavered from my intentions. Fill your mind with my Word, and you will find that peace will guide you. Fix your eyes on my goodness, and you will see it all around you.

When there is no clear prophetic vision,
people quickly wander astray.
But when you follow the revelation of the word,
heaven's bliss fills your soul.
PROVERBS 29:18

I am your portion.

B eloved, what do you need today? I have given you access to my kingdom where there is abundance for all who seek it. You have only to look to me, and I will fill you with more than you could ever imagine. I will never hesitate to lead you into my love. Where there are troubles, they will not overtake you. I am your good and faithful Father, and I won't let the difficulties you face overcome you. I will deliver you from the trap of the enemy. I will supply you with all you need in every moment.

Turn to me today and find yourself enveloped in my kindness. My delight is your gift, and I never tire of pouring it out over you. Don't stay away for fear that I will judge you harshly. You are my beloved child, and even my correction is laced with compassion. Don't be discouraged by the news you hear or the questions that remain unanswered in your life. Drink deeply of my unchanging joy and feast on my lavish love. I am your portion today and always.

Because of their faith in him,
their daily portion will be
a Father's help and deliverance from evil.
This is true for all who turn to hide themselves in him!

PSALM 37:40

You have access to more.

L et the gratitude of your heart lead you into the pursuit of more wisdom and revelation. I have so much to share with you. As you become more acquainted with my ways, you will transform into the likeness of my love. There is no shortage of revelation. What astounded you yesterday may seem commonplace today, but don't forget that I am full of truth and wisdom. The light of my understanding will make even the most mundane realities seem impossibly good.

Do not be tempted by the mentality that you have been blessed with enough and that you should feel content with what you have for fear that others will miss out. My kingdom works in a different way; there is more than enough for everyone. When you consume freely from my table of wisdom and revelation, there is more to offer others. Keep feeding the hunger of your heart by partaking in what I offer to you. Your capacity for understanding will grow as you continually listen and look with an open heart to receive. Press in and seek me out. I promise that you will find me. I'm right here!

> Everyone who listens with an open heart
> will receive progressively more revelation
> until he has more than enough.
>
> MATTHEW 13:12

My ways are better.

My child, as long as you have been drawing breath, I have seen your growth in every stage of your development. When you took your first steps, I was as proud as your parent who coaxed you. I have delighted when you discovered new ways to think about things. Who does not take joy in their children who grow into their own?

Yet what brings me even more joy is when you listen to my words of wisdom and heed my advice. They are neither empty nor do they seek to control or hem you in. I see from a different vantage point. My eyes take in every detail and the grand scope of your life as well as how it connects to those around you. I have good, good plans for you. I will not lead you somewhere I have not already gone. I am always with you. Though you cannot comprehend the enormity of my love, it is your covering all the days of your life. Spend time tuning in to my heart today. What you find will elevate your own thinking. Do you want to stay the same, or would you like to venture into new revelations today?

As high as the heavens are above the earth,
so my ways and my thoughts are higher than yours.
ISAIAH 55:9

I see it all.

B eloved, I see you clearly just as you are. I see the circumstances that are outside of your control and the troubles
knocking at your door. I see the way your heart is overwhelmed.
Do not despair and don't lose hope. I am always close. I will
bring you through this; you can count on me. When you are
afraid, put your hope in me, and when you struggle to hope,
look outside of your own experience to the fulfilled promises
of my people.

I won't let the weight of the unknown crush you. I am not
disinterested in your plight, my daughter. I will meet your
needs. Look at the way that I have come through time and again.
I have not suddenly turned my gaze from my people. When the
waters rise around you, I am your high place—your security in
the storm. Worry won't help you. Whatever it is that threatens
your peace, give it to me. I will surround you with the blanket
of my perfect peace, wrapping you up in the comfort of my love.
Come in close and rest in my steadiness. I am for you, and I will
work all things together with redemptive love for your benefit.

He will not ignore forever all the needs of the poor,
for those in need shall not always be crushed.
Their hopes shall be fulfilled, for God sees it all!

PSALM 9:18

Plant seeds of peace.

The way of wisdom is the pathway of peace. If you follow me, I will guide you along the route that leads to abundant, everlasting life. When you choose to humble yourself before others, I become your Advocate and mighty Defender. Where there is striving, let there be confident rest. You don't need to fight for yourself or make your name great. I will raise up the humble and endorse those who promote peace.

Let the ears of your heart be open to my wisdom. Lean into my ways of living. My kingdom does not look like the nations of this world. Where there are wars and battles, they will cease. Chaos and confusion mark the world's ways, but harmony defines my kingdom. When you sow peace, you will reap an eternal reward. Reflect my kindness, and the world will see that you belong to the higher way, where the law of love supersedes everything. As it has been done for you, so do for others. Choose harmony over discord and unity over selfish ambition. Choose mercy instead of vengeance, letting my love flood your heart. As you pour my mercy on others, you will find that your own peace increases.

Good seeds of wisdom's fruit will be planted with peaceful acts by those who cherish making peace.

JAMES 3:18

I am never late.

Have you grown weary of waiting on me? Don't be discouraged, daughter. I am not late. Though my timing may not make sense to you, it takes into account more than what you can see with your limited perspective.

I have always been faithful, and my character remains unchanged. Where there is worry, give it over to me. Let me breathe courage into your spirit today. Lean on me, for you can trust my intentions for your life. I am for you, and I have not abandoned you. When you see how I work all of this out for your benefit, you will understand that even a moment of worry was wasted. Rest in my faithfulness today. Meditate on my goodness. Turn your powerlessness into praise and see how your heart shifts toward trust. Do not believe those who have said that I have forgotten my people; I am still at work. Though it has been under the surface, soon you will see my power displayed before your very eyes. You can count on me to come through for you.

Say to the anxious and fearful,
"Be strong and never afraid.
Look, here comes your God!
He is breaking through to give you victory!
He comes to avenge your enemies.
With divine retribution he comes to save you!"

ISAIAH 35:4

Keep doing good.

I have declared you clean in my sight. There is nothing you need to do for me to accept you. I have welcomed you with wide-open arms. My Father-heart loves to embrace you, my child. I see how you long to reflect my goodness in your life. Don't give up on your pursuits. When you reach out to others with a heart of love, you are reflecting my life at work within you.

You have received unending measures of grace, so do not hesitate to offer it to others. When you extend mercy, you extend my heart to others. I love when you choose to partner with my compassion. Keep doing it because you can find more delight in serving those around you than by collecting temporary treasures for yourself. What you offer others will return to you, daughter. Do not feel concerned about a shortage of resources. My storehouse is overflowing, and you have free access. I delight in your heart that reaches out to others in the same way you receive from me. Clothe yourself with compassion and don't be ashamed of your mercy-heart that reveals my own. It is your strength.

Delightfully loved ones, don't imitate what is evil,
but imitate that which is good.
Whoever does good is of God;
whoever does evil has not seen God.

3 JOHN 1:11

I have the keys you need.

D aughter, search for my wisdom like you would for treasure. I will not hide myself from you. I freely give to all who sincerely seek me. My Word is full of priceless knowledge that will help you to live a life full of integrity and honor. Although few choose it, my way is better than what the world offers. It is easier to decide to hold on to resentment than to offer forgiveness. But those who choose the path of peace find that their souls remain at rest even in turmoil.

Press into my heart of love, and you will discover that I hold every key that you could ever need. I give insight to those who look for it. I offer advice and guidance to those who listen. Trust my ways and follow me, and you will live in the abundance of peace and joy. I lead you into freedom, not into bondage. As you model your life after me, your heart will expand to hold a greater capacity for love and trust. My ways are better than your own plans, and I promise that you won't be disappointed when you align your life with mine. Dig deep into my Word and find the life you've been longing for.

Within these sayings will be found the revelation of wisdom
and the impartation of spiritual understanding.
Use them as keys to unlock the treasures of true knowledge.

PROVERBS 1:2

I am your wisdom.

The Messiah-King is the hope of all the nations and your true wisdom. In me, you will find solutions to your problems and the help you need in every circumstance. I have power to do what seems impossible to your limited imagination. I can do far more than you could think to ask of me . Let me be your rock and your safe place. I will be your confident assurance.

I see every possible outcome. I am never surprised. Seek my wisdom and I will show you the best choices available to you. There is no closed door that will not open at my voice. Trust my leadership, for I won't lead you astray. I am the God of all power and all understanding, and you have unhindered access to fellowship with me. My heart is always open to you, so don't hesitate to run into my love and find the answers to your questions in my presence. Enter into my fullness that never diminishes, dear one. There is no question too simple or problem too complex—lay it all out openly before me. I will never turn you away.

For those who have been chosen to follow him,
both Jews and Greeks, he is God's mighty power,
God's true wisdom, and our Messiah.

1 CORINTHIANS 1:24

I am restoring what was lost.

W hen the dead of winter strips life to the bone, it is hard to imagine the lush growth of spring and summer. Yet even when the trees are bare and the ground is frozen, all is not lost. I will never let anything in your life go to waste. Even when heartache rips your heart in two, I will not leave you broken. I am the master restorer, and I am already doing my redemption work.

I am tenderly reviving what has been dormant, only bringing back to life that which serves you well. From the rubble of destruction, I am clearing out the unnecessary and building for you a home that lasts. Though shifting and shaking has occurred, your foundation has not moved because it is the rock of my steadfast love. Trust my kindness, daughter. I will lead you into fields growing with the bounty of my goodness. You will feast on the fruit of my faithfulness. I remain undistracted in working my purposes out in your life, and they are all for your benefit. Take my hand now, and I will remind you of the forgotten morsels of mercy in your story. I won't ever stop depositing the treasures of my kindness as long as you are drawing breath.

You brought me back from the brink of death,
from the depths below.
Now here I am, alive and well, fully restored!
PSALM 30:3

There is nothing I lack.

Y ou can find everything you look for in me. You could search the whole world for wisdom and greatness, but there is no need. You can find it here in my presence. You have full access to my storehouse of plenty. Let your heart drink deeply of my delight today. I won't let you down or let you go. I know exactly how to meet you in a meaningful way even when you don't know what it is that you're looking for. Open the eyes of your heart to receive what I have for you today.

Rest in my presence today and turn your attention toward me. You won't be disappointed in what you find. You will reach the end of yourself over and over again, but you won't ever find a limit to my love. When you are afraid, turn to me. When you cannot breathe for the worries of the world weighing you down, look to me. I will lift every burden that keeps you from living in the freedom I have offered you. You are my beloved child, and nothing can stop me from pursuing you with my fiery love. The cares of this world don't stand a chance against the joy that I have over you.

Now may God...fill you to overflowing with uncontainable joy and perfect peace as you trust in him. And may the power of the Holy Spirit continually surround your life with his super-abundance until you radiate with hope!

ROMANS 15:13

Trust my leadership.

Beloved, let today be the day you lean into my loving leadership. I won't lead you astray because my heart and intentions for you are always for your benefit and for my glory. I see the end from the beginning, and I know how to best guide you into my goodness. There is no need to struggle or to fight it, for I am trustworthy. No one can compare to my kindness. I have no hidden agenda; my affection flows through everything I do.

When you follow my gentle guidance, your feet walk on the path of righteousness. Instead of seeking to promote yourself, will you let me be your advocate? Do not despise the tendency to serve others. It is your strength and a reflection of my humble leadership. I will lift you up in due time, and no one could effectively dispute the position I give you. In the meantime, trust that every circumstance and trial is your training ground. I will raise you up, and as you stand on faith, you will see that your strength has increased every time you overcome.

The path to promotion and prominence comes by having the heart of a bond-slave who serves everyone.

MARK 10:44

Receive my delight.

No mind can comprehend the extent of my delight and my joy. Where you disappoint yourself and others, I see my daughter trying her best. There is no shame in my love, and I will never demean you or put you down. I don't ever show up in your life without the delight of you beaming from my eyes, my cherished child. It doesn't matter where you have succeeded or failed, for nothing can shake my joy over you.

Consider the way mothers see their own children. When they fall and hurt themselves, will a good mother not comfort them? When your children come to you, beaming with pride over their artful masterpieces, will you not shower them with delight and encourage them? And when they mess up, does the restoration of forgiveness not move your heart with compassion? Even so, my love is purer than the most devoted mother's. I always receive you freely when you come to me, and I am never far from you. I delight in what delights you because I love you with a full heart. Today let any hesitation in your heart melt away as you receive my pure pleasure over you.

O Lord, our God, no one can compare with you.
Such wonderful works and miracles are all found with you!
And you think of us all the time
with your countless expressions of love—
far exceeding our expectations!

PSALM 40:5

Press on in love.

Though your own resources will inevitably run dry, I am always full of abundance. My plentiful presence covers you in every season of the soul. Come to me today, and I will fill you. When your weariness leaves you feeling empty and unmotivated, let me refresh you with the power of my Spirit. I blow my reviving winds over the landscape of your heart. The rain of my mercy showers over you and restores your hope.

Keep being gracious to others. Tenderness is a gift that you can freely give away because of the abundant measure with which you've received it. Continue to stir up the passion in your heart for freedom, child. It will lead you along my path of truth and life. In me, you will always find what you are looking for, so don't give up. Nothing can thwart my plans and purposes, for I have not lost track of where I'm taking you. You can trust my intentions for your life. You can discover so much more in me. Let me remind you today of the hope to which I have called you.

I admit that I haven't yet acquired the absolute fullness that I'm pursuing, but I run with passion into his abundance so that I may reach the purpose that Jesus Christ has called me to fulfill and wants me to discover.

PHILIPPIANS 3:12

Join with my heart.

As you walk this road of life, you have an opportunity every day to partner with the purposes of my heart. My ways are steady and strong, so you can walk confidently, without fear, as you follow my example. My ways are full of loving-kindness and endless mercy. You will not find a more devoted love in this world.

The power of my affection is not weak. It puts the proud in their place and lifts the humble from the rubble of their circumstances. You cannot find true identity that lasts in your status or in ease of life—you find it in being the object of my relentless kindness. No one can talk me out of my great grace. Join with me in extending mercy to those who need it. Partner with my compassion by serving those who could never offer you anything in return. Laid-down love is the most powerful force you will ever know. You have received, so also you are called to give freely. The more you offer, the greater capacity you will have to take in. Will you take this invitation to experience more of my love by pouring out a proper portion for the fame of my name? All who see your example will know whose you are, for compassionate responses clearly reflect my character.

Yes, we will follow your ways, Lord Yahweh,
and entwine our hearts with yours,
for the fame of your name is all that we desire.

Isaiah 26:8

I am leading you into light.

There is no darkness that I won't flood with the glorious light of my presence. Even the middle of a moonless night is as clear as day to me. Do you trust me to guide you into my goodness? I will never leave you to waste away in obscurity. Where there is confusion, I bring clarity. Where there is bondage, I bring freedom.

Take my hand, daughter, and let me lead you out in peace. I will keep you safe every step of the way, and you will grow in boldness as you let me gently and confidently direct you on the path laid out before you. When you stumble, I will catch you. When you start to wander, I will redirect you. There is no fear in my love and no need to worry about missteps. You are free in me. Free to choose, free to surrender, free to be wholly you, for you are wholly loved. Where others have hemmed you in, I am breaking down walls so that you can run. As you trust me, the eyes of your heart will be enlightened so that you see me as clearly as I see you.

His light broke through the darkness and
he led us out in freedom from death's dark shadow
and snapped every one of our chains.

PSALM 107:14

Love is stronger than fear.

I n the perfection of my pure love, you will find all the courage your heart needs. Drink deeply of my kindness as I surround you with my comforting embrace today. Rest in my goodness, for there is no need to rush into action or ignore the weariness that weighs on your soul. Come to me just as you are in this moment. I meet you with my unhindered affection.

The worries of this world will not overcome you, and the grip of fear will not take you down. I overpower and disarm every anxiety. My peace is your plentiful portion—receive it today. Come to the waters of my resting place where I will refresh you with my luxurious love. I will revive your life with my healing peace until your heart overflows with my Spirit's fruit. You have no room for fear when you are full of the confident pursuit of my goodness and love over your life. My presence is the seal of my promise to you. Surrender today to my overwhelming affection that purifies your heart and brings clarity and courage.

Lord, even when your path takes me through
the valley of deepest darkness,
fear will never conquer me, for you already have!
You remain close to me…
The comfort of your love takes away my fear.

PSALM 23:4

I am easy to please.

Beloved, whenever you approach my throne of grace, my heart overflows with love that pours out over your life. I have not withheld my kindness from you for even a moment. Come close and taste my fresh mercy again. Let your heart unfold in the light of my glory and goodness. My faithfulness has marked every piece of your story, and it is still at work.

When you feel discouragement set in, draw near and let me lift it like a veil. You will see that my truth brings a refreshing perspective to even the harshest circumstances. Instead of trying harder to gain my favor, turn to me, and I will show you that I am already as proud as I'll ever be. Your willing and pliant heart is a testimony of my life in yours. Every glance my way and every consideration of my Word brings me great joy. Even when you doubt your own goodness, I do not. You reflect me in the ways you reach out in love and self-sacrifice. I am continually molding you to my image, child, and your freedom is increasing as you see my kindness knit into your being. Drink deeply of my delight today.

When people turn to you,
they discover how easy you are to please—so faithful and true!
Joyfully you teach them the proper path,
even when they go astray.

PSALM 25:8

Listen to my voice.

As my child, you know my voice. You have recognized my still, sure voice in the quiet of your soul. My words, laced in love, have led you further into freedom every step of the way. Do you forget that I am a good Father? I am not silent, daughter. Lean into my loving heart and hear the words of life that fill you with the courage you need. My guidance is always with your benefit in mind. If you choose to listen, you will not be disappointed.

My wisdom is the treasure you seek. Therefore don't be fooled into thinking that the world's ways are better. They will leave you dissatisfied in the end. When you struggle to choose, love, let me wash over you with my kindness and remind you that my heart is full of generosity and goodness. I am not a dictator but a loving Counselor. My loyal lovers will find true success in following the advice I freely give. I will never force you to follow me, and I won't remove my mercy from your life if you choose a different way. I see how your heart longs for fulfillment, daughter, and you will find that in me. Align your life with mine and find the freedom and joy that heeding my wisdom brings.

When you turn to the right or turn to the left,
you will hear his voice behind you to guide you, saying,
"This is the right path; follow it."

ISAIAH 30:21

Nothing is impossible.

All things are possible when you believe in me. You can take me at my Word. My promises are true, and I will always follow through on my intentions. My loving-kindness will never, ever fail you. Where in your life do you feel hemmed in? Invite me into it, beloved. Let me give you my higher perspective so that you can see where I am already at work turning the tide. No barrier can stand up against the rushing river of my mercy.

I always make a way where there seems to be none. When you cannot see a possibility for breakthrough, let your focus shift from your own understanding to seeing with the eyes of faith. Would you dare believe that the same God who split the seas so that the Israelites could escape the bondage of Egypt will make a way for you? I will do it. Dig into my Word and to the power of the testimony of my faithfulness in the lives of my beloved ones. What I have done for others, I will do for you— and even more. Let confident assurance increase in your heart as you trust in me.

Yahweh is the one who makes a way in the sea,
a pathway in the mighty waters.

ISAIAH 43:16

Trust my wisdom.

Dearest daughter, do not hesitate in my presence in this moment. Come close as I lean into your heart with wisdom that will fill you with strength for today. I never withhold from those who truly long for understanding. I see your questioning, and you can be free with me. Lay it all out there. As you open your heart, you will find that my heart is unrestricted toward you. You have full access to the fullness of my mercy.

Though you vacillate in your opinion from day to day, my truth remains constant through the ages. You can rely on my perspective to guide you into my goodness at every turn. Though you may fall a hundred times, I will pick you up every single time. It does not matter what yesterday looked like. Today is the day I have given you, and I am full of affection over you as your good and faithful Father. Trust my words of wisdom to lead you in love. That is the way of my kingdom.

If anyone longs to be wise, ask God for wisdom and he will give it! He won't see your lack of wisdom as an opportunity to scold you over your failures but he will overwhelm your failures with his generous grace.

JAMES 1:5

There's no better time.

Today is the day I have given you. Have you been ruminating over the failures of the past? Have you been rushing ahead in your plans? Let the power of yesterday's regrets dissipate in the warmth of my very-present love. Let the questions about tomorrow rest in the palm of my hand as you lean into this moment where you and I are one. Ground yourself in my truth as I speak my words of life over you. You have everything you need for all that you face today. I am your sustenance and your provider. Nothing that you come up against is outside of my knowledge. I have equipped you with all you require.

You are a reflection of a generous king. When it is in your power to graciously give to others, do not put it off until another time. Do what you know to do when it is at hand. My wisdom is better than the world's, and I will not lead you astray. When you choose to sow seeds in laid-down love, the return will always be sweet. Continue to persevere in kindness and compassion, for there is no better time than the present.

When your friend comes to ask you for a favor, why would you say, "Perhaps tomorrow," when you have the money right there in your pocket? Help him today!

PROVERBS 3:28

Listen to my heart.

Come close and listen to the wisdom I have to offer you. There is understanding to expand your perspective and give you clarity of vision for whatever lies in front of you. I have more than enough revelation to fill your mind every moment of every day for the rest of your existence. However, there is no pressure to gorge on truth. Come and be satisfied. Be filled. Some truth is like water, easily going down. Other times, it is like a rich dessert, where a couple of bites are more than enough to satisfy.

There is no need to live off of yesterday's bread, child. I have a fresh Word for you today. Open wide and receive freely what it is I am offering. The more you practice listening, the quicker you will respond to my voice. How it delights me when you press into my heart and listen for my voice. Even now, I have exactly what you don't even know you need. Follow me into the sanctuary of my presence, where you will find treasures beyond your wildest imaginings. Come and see! Taste and eat my wonderful wisdom, and you will be gratified.

Train your heart to listen when I speak
and open your spirit wide to expand your discernment—
then pass it on to your sons and daughters.

PROVERBS 2:2

See from a higher perspective.

I am full of wisdom for all who seek it and understanding for those willing to listen. I have not ever misled you or hidden my heart from you. I am full of truth, for I am the living Word. I invite you to look at life from my vantage point. Your heart will gain comprehension when you catch a glimpse of what I see.

Just as I instructed Samuel, so I will say the same to you today. You may judge another by outward appearance, but I look straight to the heart. No one can see a heart's intricacies except for me, and only I know the true intentions of a person's will. You will have to trust that I know better and that I take into consideration all the things you cannot see. My character will never waver in compassion. So follow me in my merciful way, and you will bear the fruit of honor and integrity as you live in line with my kingdom's purposes and values. All who know you will taste the fruit of my goodness as you align your heart with my own!

They said to Jesus, "Teacher, we know that you're an honest man of integrity and you teach us the truth of God's ways. ... You're not one who speaks only to win the people's favor, because you speak the truth without regard to the consequences."

MATTHEW 22:16

Be rooted in love.

L et my tender love be the source that feeds your life. My mercy is strong enough to cover every weakness. In fact, my great grace takes the frail things of creation and makes them more fruitful than the most efficient systems of the world. Be strengthened by the sustenance of my great kindness that heals all of your wounds and restores every broken dream.

You choose well when you opt to stand on the firm foundation of my never-failing love. No storm can crack my immoveable groundwork under your feet. You will never want for anything when you wade in the waters of my complete compassion. When winds blow, they will only cause greater waves of my mercy to wash over you. You cannot escape the reaches of my affection, so do the best thing and burrow yourself into me. The resulting growth will be worth more than a hundred lifetimes in self-service. Be encouraged as you dig deep into my heart today. Let the rushing river of my presence flood your senses with my goodness.

Your spiritual roots go deeply into his life as you are continually infused with strength, encouraged in every way. For you are established in the faith you have absorbed and enriched by your devotion to him!

Colossians 2:7

Your purpose is found here.

B eloved, do not forget that your identity is firmly rooted in my love for you. I created you with pleasure, and it is my delight when you live in the freedom of your purpose as my daughter. It brings me great joy when you stand in the strength of who I say you are. Live unapologetically in the light of my love. Don't let others who would only cut you down diminish your confidence. My tender affection completely covers you. There is no need to ration my kindness, for it is always overflowing.

Let your feet lead you into the dance of unhindered joy. Let your unrestrained worship reflect the passion of your heart. Lead the way, daughter, with your beautiful song rising to the heavens. The beauty found in fields of blooming flowers has nothing on your passionate praise. The fragrance of your offerings is more pleasing than the finest perfumes of the elite. The treasure of your adoration is more valuable than the fortune of the richest kingdoms on earth. How incredibly cherished you are, my beloved one!

Everything you have made will praise you, fulfilling its purpose.
And all your godly lovers will be found bowing before you.

PSALM 145:10

My presence is your sustenance.

Those who rest in me are continually renewed. No matter how weary and weak you are, come to me, child, and find the refreshing your soul needs. I have love in abundance to pour over you. Drink deeply of the joy my presence produces in you. My peace steadies even the most fragile hope. Whatever it is you long for today, you will find its fullness in me.

My Spirit fills you with the kindness of my heart so that you can truly understand and know that I am for you. Be strengthened by the boldness of my love as I surround you with my wraparound presence. Let the troubles of your heart come to peace as I speak my words of life over you. Worries lose their power when my faithfulness shines on you. Just look and see! I am as constant in compassion as I have ever been. I equip you with everything you need for a life of abundance in my love. Behold, I am with you, and I am producing sweet, satisfying fruit in the garden of your heart.

The fruit produced by the Holy Spirit within you is divine love in all its varied expressions: joy that overflows, peace that subdues, patience that endures, kindness in action, a life full of virtue, faith that prevails, gentleness of heart, and strength of spirit.

GALATIANS 5:22–23

I am your guide.

B eloved, do not be afraid and do not despair. When the path you walk becomes rough and unsteady, I will support you with my strong right hand. I promise to guide you through every trial. I have not left you alone, and I never will. Don't let the uncertainties of this life cause doubt to sweep you away. Confusion spins everything so that even what is steady seems unstable. But my peace brings every chaotic thought to rest, and even the unruliest messes come back into order.

I smooth out the most difficult roads with my grace. My mercy fills in every crack along the way. You will not be lost to darkness, for I am light, and I am with you. I bring clarity to every mystery and confident assurance with my faithfulness. Trust and do not dismay. Whatever comes, I see it all, and I am by your side. I promise to work all things to benefit you, but you will have to trust that my ways are higher than your own. As long as it is called *today*, I have got you.

I will walk the blind by an unknown way
and guide them on paths they've never traveled.
I will smooth their difficult road
and make their dark mysteries bright with light. ...
For I will never abandon my beloved ones.

Isaiah 42:16

No time to waste.

D o you feel as if your days are fleeting? Time will pass whether you're paying attention or not. How are you using your days, beloved? Practicing the habit of being tuned to the present is how you can take hold of the time you have. The past is behind you though you can learn from it. The future is ahead, and it can be a driving force that keeps you going, but it can also distract from what you have here and now. Don't forget to pay attention to the present moment.

Practice presence, beloved. Be aware of what you are giving your attention to. Train your thoughts by grounding them in truth. Anchor your mind by tuning in to my presence. This is the moment I have given you. Will you let it race by, or will you give it intention? Let your life align with my love as you set your heart on practicing purposeful presence with those around you. You have received a gift in this life, and it is not too late to be diligent in purpose. Take your thoughts captive, love, and you will find that joy is already here in this present season.

Lord, help me to know how fleeting my time on earth is.
Help me to know how limited is my life
and that I'm only here but for a moment more.

PSALM 39:4

My Word is trustworthy.

You can count on me to work out my promises in your life. What I say, I will do. Follow my faithfulness through the ages and you will see that no matter what circumstances say, I am always operating and following through on my word. Beloved, let your heart take hope in my loyal love today. I am constant and true, and you will see the light of my life breaking through for you.

What are your hopes set on this day? What is your heart depending on? Come into the sanctuary of my presence where my glory lights up every shadow. This place relieves the pressure of doubt. Let the breath of my Word fill you with the strength you need to live a life of abundant love. I promise that I will never leave you or forsake you. I am leading you along the path of my mercy that leads to everlasting life and freedom. Feast on my Word as a famished child would devour her bread. I have promised that the hungry will be satisfied, so eat and find that your desire for me grows with each bite.

Every Scripture has been written by the Holy Spirit, the breath of God. It will empower you by its instruction and correction, giving you the strength to take the right direction and lead you deeper into the path of godliness.

2 TIMOTHY 3:16

February

I am here still.

Beloved, I see how you have journeyed through the valley of the shadow of death. You started out strong in faith and believing that I was with and for you. Though this season has lasted longer than you imagined it would, I see how your heart wrestles to hold out hope. Do not despair, my child. I have not left you alone, and I did not step away, even for a second. I have been here all along—let me show you.

Where disappointment has set in, don't get settled into it. I am bringing you out of the valley into an open field full of light and life. Where you have felt trapped, you will know the release of openness and space once again. When you look back, you will see that new growth and beauty fill the path where you once walked in darkness and confusion.

The shadows have taught you to trust my leadership and to know my voice, my touch, and my character. Though you may have questioned my goodness for a moment, you will see that it has always been your covering and your faithful companion. There is a new door opening—can you see it? Keep pressing into me, for I will be your comfort and strength. We're almost there!

Because you are close to me and always available,
my confidence will never be shaken,
for I experience your wrap-around presence every moment.

PSALM 16:8

I am your joy.

Darling daughter, there is fullness of joy in my presence. Run into the sunshine of my love today and don't hold back. I will never turn away a thirsty soul. Drink deeply of my delight as I reveal my compassion to you in a fresh way. Are you still clinging to blessings from the past? I have more to offer you here and now. I promise that as you follow me, you will find more freedom in my joy than you have ever known in your own capacity.

My intentions for you are good, my child. As you align your life with my Word, you will find yourself walking the pathway of peace, full of light and life. When you fellowship with my Spirit, you will find that you have the abundance of heaven's treasures at your fingertips. My wisdom is more valuable than all the world's gold, and you can have as much of it as you seek out. I will never withhold my goodness from you. Press in, and delight will fill you as I turn even your darkest days into a treasure trove of my goodness.

I find more joy in following what you tell me to do
than in chasing after all the wealth of the world.

PSALM 119:14

I invite you into my love.

In fellowship with me, you have access to abounding love that never lets up or lets go. Fullness of affectionate joy resides in my presence. Communion with my Spirit has invited you into my goodness. I have closed the distance, daughter. Nothing can separate you from my commanding kindness. It saturates you.

And yet, there is more. My love is a never-ending flow that rushes straight from my heart over your life. Look and see the evidence of my generous mercy through my Son's example and testimony. Do you see my faithfulness, how it doesn't ever give up? Do you sense the reality of my goodness in your life? If you're finding it hard to see me in your present circumstances, look up and around. I don't ever leave my loyal lovers to waste away. Dig into my Word and find the hope of generations feasting on my faithfulness. You are an heir to the same promises. Let me lovingly lead you into truth as you receive the delight of my heart.

I have revealed to them who you are
and I will continue to make you even more real to them,
so that they may experience the same endless love
that you have for me,
for your love will now live in them, even as I live in them!

JOHN 17:26

I have brought you in.

As a beloved child, you have been welcomed into my kingdom with the full delight of heaven. You do not need to worry about anything with the King of kings as your provider. You are an heir of the living God and a harbinger of my presence on the earth. There is so much joy over your identity as my child. Let your own heart rejoice in this reality.

Have you forgotten the glorious goodness of being alive to your distinct status as partner with my heart? Let me remind you what's in store for those who live under my goodness. There is eternal glory that will never dwindle in my presence, and you have free access. Don't hesitate to come to me with whatever you need. Your hopes won't be disappointed when they're set on me. And even when questions arise, I do not turn you away. I will reveal the truth behind every mystery when the time is right. There is fullness of everlasting joy in me, and you will experience delight that never fades, even into eternity.

As a result, the kingdom's gates will open wide to you as God choreographs your triumphant entrance into the eternal kingdom of our Lord and Savior, Jesus the Messiah.

2 PETER 1:11

I am writing your story.

Just as an author puts pen to paper and creates worlds with her words, so have I created the world within which you live. Your character is being shaped, and your story is unfolding just as it should be. As you walk through this life, I am creating a pathway for you with each twist and turn in the plot.

I see the bigger picture of your life because I am not limited in my perspective. Trust that I won't let the tensions of heartache and hardship be the end of your story. Here in the trouble is where the most beautiful transformations take place. I am already working it out for your benefit. Let me show you the beautiful tapestry that I am weaving from the different threads of your life. I will waste nothing. Even what seems unbearable, I will turn to beauty in my hands. You don't believe me? Watch me do it.

You cannot convince me to leave you alone or to give up on you. Instead, lean back into my love and give yourself over to the overwhelming joy that I have for you. Feast on my love and find life in the courage of your faith.

Wherever I go, your hand will guide me;
your strength will empower me.
It's impossible to disappear from you
or to ask the darkness to hide me,
for your presence is everywhere, bringing light into my night.

PSALM 139:10–11

My heart is full of love.

Beloved, my love is a never-ending flow of pure, living water straight from the source of my heart. It never ebbs. It flows over the land of your heart and brings life to everything it touches. So much more than you can imagine is available for all who live and breathe.

The intentions of my plans hold the universe in place. I have not forgotten what I foretold long ago—not a word will go wasted. I am not slow in fulfilling my promises. I see the seasons and signs of the times. I am waiting for the right moment, when all conditions are optimal for successful growth. I know exactly when to plant the seeds, when to prune, and when to harvest. Don't worry about where you are in the process—I've got you. You will thrive in the environment in which I've planted you, and I will protect you when the storms come. Remember that I take all factors into consideration, and what you see as wasted time is for your good and your protection. Trust me, daughter. It will all work out in my perfect timing. Rest in my love in the meantime and let it carry you through every season.

Lord, your nurturing love is tender and gentle.
You are slow to get angry yet so swift to show your faithful love.
You are full of abounding grace and truth.

PSALM 86:15

Come to the table.

Don't hesitate to come to my table of plenty today. Everything you could ever need I have laid out before you. Come and eat. Feast on the abundance of my love—it is yours for the taking. There is no need to circle my table, waiting for scraps to fall your way. I have reserved a seat for you by my side. As my child, you are always welcome here.

It's time to shut down the lies of shame that have kept you from freely receiving my grace and mercy. I have already set you free from the chains of sin that held you back, so don't put yourself back into a place of scarcity because of your failures and shortcomings. I have covered you with my grace and torn the thick curtain that kept you out of my courts. There is no more separation, only unhindered connection. I promise that I will never turn you away. I delight in your presence more than you could ever delight in mine. Come in close and find fruitful fellowship with my Spirit today. Lift your gaze to mine and look into my eyes filled with fiery love that burns away all shame and doubt. You'll find that you already have everything you need here in me.

Worship in awe and wonder, all you who've been made holy!
For all who fear him will feast with plenty.

PSALM 34:9

Do not despair.

D aughter, I offer you great confidence as you rest in me. Lean back into my loving arms and let me show you just how reliable I am. Let me refresh you in the atmosphere of my peace. Though troubles come into your life, I am the conqueror of all that produces sin and death. My power at work in your life will leave you amazed at every turn, for I never abandon my loyal lovers.

Do you not remember my faithfulness? Let me give you proper perspective, love. Look through the lens of my unfailing mercy that stretches from ages past into the eternal future. Take your courage in my reliable kindness, for it covers you all the days of your life. My perfect peace is your portion every day. Enter into the rest of my presence, and I will encourage your soul in the refreshing pool of my compassion. You will find your strength renewed with your faith rooted in my faithfulness.

Everything I've taught you is so that the peace which is in me will be in you and will give you great confidence as you rest in me. For in this unbelieving world you will experience trouble and sorrows, but you must be courageous, for I have conquered the world!

JOHN 16:33

Let me encourage you.

C ome into the secret place and find encouragement that waters your thirsty soul. I have words of life to share with you today and living-understanding to strengthen you. Run into the shelter of my presence and let my love wash over you in a fresh way. I don't offer stale bread to my hungry lovers. Eat of my *now* word. Tune your ear to my voice.

Give me the heavy weight of the burden of fear you are carrying. There may be uncertainty in your life, but I see everything clearly. There are no mysteries to me, and I won't let the tides of confusion sweep you away. See how my hand holds you steady. You cannot escape the grip of my glorious grace, child. What wondrous plans I have for you. What a future you have in me. Let me guide you further into my goodness as you follow my leading. I promise never to let you go or get too far ahead. I give you eyes to see from my perspective. Look to me, and nothing will ever shatter your hope.

You will find true success when you find me,
for I have insight into wise plans that are designed just for you.
I hold in my hands living-understanding, courage, and strength.

PROVERBS 8:14

Give me your attention.

Daughter, you cannot comprehend the lengths my love goes to reach you. There is not a moment when my mercy separates from you. Lean into my heart of compassion today and find life in the rhythms of my grace. I will share with you the secrets of my heart as you look to me.

Let my wisdom instruct your ways. Let my perspective shape your habits, and you will find that your character becomes like my own. The qualifications of my lovers are willing hearts and humble attitudes. When you choose to trust me, even in the wilderness of confusion, you strengthen the cord of faith that will sustain you. Look to me, child, and give me your attention. I will fill you with the strength and encouragement your soul longs for. Though you cannot imagine how deep my kindness goes, you are swimming in its depths. Let my waves of love crash over you as you let go of the worries of today.

The Lord looks down in love,
bending over heaven's balcony,
looking over all of Adam's sons and daughters.
He's looking to see if there is anyone who acts wisely,
any who are searching for God and wanting to please him.

PSALM 14:2

Find your pleasure in my own.

My heart is full of gladness today. Let my joy fill your soul with encouragement and life. I did not design life to deplete you of delight since pleasure is knit into your very framework. Be free today in my abundant love. There is no need to meter out your own joy. Become like a child again and let your delight lead you. If you are having trouble remembering how to lay down your responsibilities and just be free in my love, let me remind you.

When you were a girl, you knew how to embrace what brought you joy. It is time to channel your inner child and let your innocent wildness out to play. Your laughter brings light to my eyes, and your smile is more radiant than a thousand sunsets. There's no need to be so solemn, my love. Let the heaviness lift from your shoulders as you dance in my delight. Don't waste another moment waiting to receive my pure pleasure. Nothing you could do could make me love you more, and nothing could make me love you less. You are my cherished one.

My purpose for telling you these things is so that the joy that
I experience will fill your hearts with overflowing gladness!

JOHN 15:11

Be true.

B eloved one, you are the apple of my eye and a pure reflection of my absolute delight. When your life aligns with the truth of my Word, there are treasures untold to be mined within the details of your story. I am not a man that I would lie—I am true to my Word at every turn. You can trust that what I say, I do.

In the same way, be true, daughter. Reflect the truth of my own heart in choosing to be honest whenever you have the opportunity. There is no need to hide the beauty of my life within yours. Don't complicate my ways, love. It is simple. Let love be the anthem of your life: live truly, seek me with all of your heart, and serve others out of compassion. I will honor every honest stand you take and the humility of your heart that seeks to understand. Do not be dogmatic but be aligned with life. You need not fear the repercussions of being true, daughter. There are no threads of lies to unravel in the lives of my authentic and free lovers.

Truthful words will stand the test of time,
but one day every lie will be seen for what it is.

PROVERBS 12:19

Winter won't last forever.

Every season has a beginning and an end. Nature is cyclical, and so is your life. You are not lost to an eternal winter where you struggle to see growth. Soon the winter winds will turn into spring rains, and the earth will be primed for renewal. There is beauty in the barrenness of winter that prepares you for the joy of spring, even if it's difficult to see. New life does not appear out of nothing. In order to make room for the new, the old must pass away. Do not despise the in-between.

Spring is most assuredly on its way, but here and now, I am working behind the scenes of your life. Don't wish away this present moment, for I am still the same God who abundantly pours out my love over you in every turn of your heart. Turn your attention to me now, and I will give you a glimpse into my very present goodness. There's no need to wait another moment to taste and see that I am completely and wholly for you. Lean in, love!

Every dry and barren place will burst forth with abundant blossoms,
dancing and spinning with delight! …
My people will see the awesome glory of Yahweh,
the beautiful grandeur of our God.

ISAIAH 35:2

All are welcome in me.

C reation is a reflection of my all-encompassing beauty. Look with the eyes of my creativity and see the diversity of people and landscapes around you. I never make the same thing twice. You are uniquely and wonderfully made, just as every other living creature is distinct in its own right. Don't ever give in to the idea that different is undesirable, for all things find their origin in me.

Where you have found your home in my love, there is room for all to abide. Clothe yourself in my compassion and you will know the vastness of my love. Extend kindness where others might turn a cold shoulder. When you welcome others with open arms, you reflect the same kind of reception you receive from me. In my mercy, you have found complete acceptance, and it is the same offer I make to all who look to me. Be found like me by exercising the same gracious motion of love that you have watched me pour out time and again. Be a voice of my kindheartedness to all who will listen!

The foreigner who joins himself to Yahweh
should never say,
"Because I'm a foreigner,
Yahweh will exclude me from his people."
And the eunuchs should never say,
"Because I can't have children, I'm just a barren tree."

ISAIAH 56:3

I am able.

L ean into my wisdom today as I speak my words of life over you. Do you think that my mercy makes me weak? That my tender love means that I am vulnerable? Don't be misled, my daughter. My compassion is stronger than all of the earth's armies combined. My love is not frail, and neither is yours. Surrender to the flow of my gracious tide. Let your faith reflect the confidence of my power at work. My character is your strength, so fill your mind with my ways. Let my unfailing nature take your thoughts captive.

It is not difficult for me to turn the current of your heart. So will you bind your hopes to my faithfulness? Will you trust my kindness to break through in every area where you feel stuck? I can do anything for you, daughter. I am singing freedom songs over you even now. Lean in and hear the melodies of heaven raining over your life. I am your strong and mighty tower, your Advocate and Defender. I am your faithful Father and your persistent comfort. I will never let you go or let you down.

It's as easy for God to steer a king's heart for his purposes
as it is for him to direct the course of a stream.

PROVERBS 21:1

Take me at my word.

The power of my living Word is at work in the world around you. Your life cannot escape the faithfulness of my promises. You are not on the outside of my purposes, beloved. Let your heart take hope as you trust in my unending mercy that completely covers you. My powerful presence wraps around you and sustains you in every season. I will never abandon you or take my presence from you.

Just as flowers break through the ground after spring rains, so will your hope spring up as my living waters of redeeming grace refresh you. My Word is my covenant, and it cannot be broken. Trust that what I have spoken, I will accomplish. I will not fail you, and I won't throw my hands into the air and give up. My relentless love always pursues my people. Nothing can talk me out of my marvelous mercy. I am the great I AM. All power and authority is mine. I am Creator, and I am Sustainer. Hide yourself in me today, for I am your very present help and the lifter of your head.

The earth and sky will wear out and fade away before one word
I speak loses its power or fails to accomplish its purpose.

MATTHEW 24:35

There is purpose in the valley.

B eloved, do not be discouraged by the experience of your humanity. Even Jesus subjected himself to the depths of the human experience, with loss, suffering, and hardship. And yet his life revealed a higher way of living. Uninterrupted communion with me was a gift that you could not have imagined before him, and yet here you are living in the blessing of it. There is not even a thin veil that separates my Spirit from you. You get to experience the fullness of my love at all times.

It's time to look over your history with me and remember all that I've brought you through up until now. And don't stop there—study the Scriptures and see how I lead my people through impossible situations. I never fail to consistently show up in faithful mercy. Whatever you face, either now or in the future, is another opportunity to see my redemptive power at work. Beloved, look through the lens of my perfect wisdom, and I will give you perspective to see what I am doing. You can trust that I am always with you. I never leave!

All the tests they endured on their way through the wilderness are a symbolic picture, an example that provides us with a warning so that we can learn through what they experienced. For . . . the purpose of all the ages past is now completing its goal within us.

1 CORINTHIANS 10:11

Let love bring you together.

Draw near and hear what I am speaking today. There is no unity of Spirit without community, for how can one be divided against itself? You have been born to a body of believers, a family of kingdom warriors. Don't let pointless feuds distract you from the one thing that I have called you to do: to love. Let your heart remain humble as you choose to extend forgiveness to those who have wronged you. Let the mercy of my love permeate your choice to vulnerably join with others in my purposes.

You know by now that perfection is not the goal of following me. You have walked the road of my kindness that has revealed that compassion, more than dogma, is my way of leadership. I am your perfect leader and the only wise God. In the body of believers is where you get to practice all that I taught through Jesus. Do not let pride or offense keep you from meeting together. Let my mercy wash over your heart afresh and give you the perspective of my living Word.

I'm asking you, my friends, that you be joined together in perfect unity—with one heart, one passion, and united in one love. Walk together with one harmonious purpose and you will fill my heart with unbounded joy.

PHILIPPIANS 2:2

Your lifestyle is your worship.

A s children model the behavior of their parents, so do you become like that which you admire. When you emulate my character in your life, it is the highest form of worship you could offer. Look at your lifestyle, beloved. What does your love look like? You reflect me when you choose to offer mercy instead of revenge, humility instead of selfish ambition, and compassion instead of ire. It is never too late to align your life with mine.

Don't feel discouraged when you see areas that fall short, for I have everything you need to rise up and follow me. I will teach you my ways. As long as you seek after me, you will see the fruit of my goodness in your life. My character will reflect in your own choices as you live with a grateful heart that continually chooses the law of love. Nothing is more sacred than a surrendered life. What a fragrant offering it is. As the object of my delight, you cannot ever overestimate what joy you bring me. Draw near now and let your hope come alive in my marvelous mercy.

Beloved friends, what should be our proper response to God's marvelous mercies? I encourage you to surrender yourselves to God to be his sacred, living sacrifices. And live in holiness, experiencing all that delights his heart. For this becomes your genuine expression of worship.

ROMANS 12:1

Follow through.

Your word has sealed whatever you have vowed to do. Do everything in your power to follow through on it. When the going gets hard, lean into my love for the strength to press on. There is a season to sow and a season to reap, and I am the season keeper. If you are looking for wisdom, you will find it in me. If you have any questions, lay them out without restraint. I will answer you.

Listen to me, child. If you are looking for a way out, you will find it. My loyal lovers know that the easy way is not the same as the right way. Do not look with the eyes of this world that seek a swift solution to discomfort. I am asking you to align with my wisdom that leads you in perfect peace, whatever the condition of the path. Perseverance is a marker of faith in action. When the temptation arises to give up on the good that you set out to do, remember that my unfailing mercy never gives up. Clothe yourself in humility and integrity, and follow my lead as you faithfully fulfill your responsibilities.

You should finish what you started.
You were so eager in your intentions to give, so go do it.
Finish this act of worship according to your ability to give.

2 Corinthians 8:11

I am reading your heart.

As a scholar takes in the knowledge of her texts, so I read you like a book, my dear one. I see straight through the outer layers directly to your heart. You don't have to fear what I find when I look at you. I am not surprised. Let me shine my glory light on the shadows you have been skirting around. There is nothing to be apprehensive about—trust me.

I will pour out the honey of my mercy over your heart as I teach you a better way to live. What has kept you stuck need not be a coping tool any longer. My love is strong enough to conquer the grave; surely you can trust that it is enough to heal the wounds in your heart. I will not fail you. Remember that my wisdom's ways lead you along paths of peace for my name's sake. I see the longings that have been left unsatisfied, and I will quench each one with the living water of my Word. My faithfulness is undeniable, and I won't let you down, daughter. Open up and let the light in as I revive your hope today!

> He is closely watching everything that happens.
> And with a glance, his eyes examine every heart.
> For his heavenly rule will prevail over all.
>
> Psalm 11:4

You are fully accepted.

D raw near to my heart, child, and find the full acceptance you long for. Let the light of my pure presence shine on your inner world even now. See how I delight over you. There is not a hint of disappointment in my view of you. I have enfolded you into my family, and I love you purely and wholly, just as you are.

Let the embrace of my affection wrap around you as you look to me. Let my words of life drench your spirit with the fragrant oil of my goodness. Leave behind your disenchantment as you follow me to my pools of pleasure. You have not lost your hope, my beloved. It is right here, in the exchange of my perspective for your own. It is my joy to restore you. Even now, will you remember the confident expectation that your soul knew in the days of great faith? You now have even more courage within you. Just watch and see what I have done and what I will do for you. Bind your will to mine and be free in your true identity as my beloved daughter.

You did not receive the "spirit of religious duty," leading you back into the fear *of never being good enough*. But you have received the "Spirit of full acceptance," enfolding you into the family of God.

ROMANS 8:15

Shame has no place here.

B eloved daughter, I have purified your heart in the cleansing fire of my love. I have fully restored you to life in the waterfall of my mercy. Do not let the chains of shame wrap around your mind and entrap you in cycles of disgrace. I have declared you free from your sin, and now it's time to throw off the chains that I have already loosed.

You have heard that I am the God of restoration. Now taste and see that it is true for you. Your destiny and my redemptive plan intertwine. Nothing can hold you down except for the lies that you agree with. Lift your eyes to mine and see the pure love shining from them. I am not disappointed in you, child. You are my beloved one, and I have destined you for joy and freedom in every season your soul encounters. Leave all your pride and shame at the door of my throne room. Where my presence reaches, mercy covers you. Take a deep breath and feel the weight lifted off your chest. I have set you free, so you are free indeed.

You open the eyes of the blind
and you fully restore those bent over with shame.
You love those who love and honor you.

PSALM 146:8

Reach out in hope.

Today, no matter what you're feeling, you have an invitation to more freedom in my presence. Come close and find me. I have not left you to waste away under the weight of worry; come into my pleasant presence and drink in the delight of my heart. You can trust me to take care of every detail of your life. I see it all, so lay it down and find rest.

Listen closely and you will hear the playful invitation to find pleasure in me today. I still hold the world and see all of its woes, so you don't have to keep count of it yourself. Breathe deeply of my delight as you follow my voice. I have so much to share with you. Nothing can steal your joy when you find it in my abundant presence. Let me remind you today what hope feels like. Be refreshed in the stream of my joy as you fellowship with my Spirit. Only reach out, child, and let me pull you into the pool of my love that revives your weary soul.

Here I am depressed and downcast.
Yet I will still remember you as I ponder the place
where your glory streams down from the mighty mountaintops,
lofty and majestic—the mountains of your awesome presence.

PSALM 42:6

Let your faith grow.

In the soil of my strong love, the roots of your faith have gone deep. In times of testing, you have not shown flimsy hope. The storms that shook the circumstances in your life pushed more of the growth under the surface. What you could not comprehend at the time was that this was preparing you to be strengthened and fruitful in any season. Look through my lens of grace today, and you will see my goodness has never left you. You could never elude the embrace of my faithful mercy.

I am inviting you into even deeper trust and greater reliance on me today. Tune into my Spirit that is living and active within you. I will give you revelation of my kindness that has been tending to the garden of your heart all along. There is no height that my love does not tower over. There is no depth that my compassion does not reach beyond. You are firmly rooted in my affectionate friendship, so stand tall in the confidence of our fellowship.

Faith brings our hopes into reality and becomes the foundation needed to acquire the things we long for. It is all the evidence required to prove what is still unseen.

HEBREWS 11:1

My love is steady.

Beloved, stand tall upon the firm foundation of my loving nature. My mercy is rock-solid, and it cannot be moved. Look to me today and know that I already have my eye on you. It doesn't matter how motivated you are today or how connected your heart feels. My love is unshakeable—no, it never wavers.

Let your expectation increase as you remember that I am your confidence. My faithfulness is more dependable than the North Star, so you can confidently put all your hopes in my steady nature. Give me what you have, and I will pour out my abundance on you. Do you need more peace? I've got a plentiful portion that is all yours. My presence will offer you incredible strength to keep pressing on in love. The current of my kindness will carry you through every obstacle in your path. Do not fear what tomorrow will bring; my understanding is complete, and my wisdom is unmatched. I will not let dread overtake you, for I have overcome every possible disaster with my resurrection power. Not even the grave can stop my love. Wait in hope, knowing that I will always come through for you.

The eyes of the Lord are upon
even the weakest worshipers who love him—
those who wait in hope and expectation
for the strong, steady love of God.

PSALM 33:18

My presence heals.

Come rest in the embrace of my endless kindness today. Let me surround you with the presence of my perfect peace that quiets the chaos of a busy mind. My peace stills the raging storms of hatred. It brings healing to the most fatal wounds. Whatever your state, you are not too far gone. The miracle works of Jesus are but a foretaste of what I will do for and through you. Healing is yours, child, for you belong to me.

I am your strong defense and the rock foundation of your faith. I have anointed you with the same Spirit that anointed my Son. The life-giving power of my marvelous mercy fills you. Even now, I am drawing you into deeper fellowship with me and into the intimacy of the exchange of my delight for yours, which brings me more joy than I can express. I wrap you up in my delight. As you continue your emotional and physical healing, you resemble my likeness more and more. You can trust that I will continue to instruct you in the way you should go and in the ministry of my lavish love.

Jesus of Nazareth was anointed by God with the Holy Spirit
and with great power. He did wonderful things for others
and divinely healed all who were under the tyranny of the devil,
for God had anointed him.

ACTS 10:38

Fellowship is a gift.

B eloved, I created you for companionship. Communion is your birthright. I did not form you with the objective that you would rely only on yourself in life. Think of the way you came into this world: you were vulnerable, relying on your caregivers to provide for every need. And yet it goes so much deeper than that, child. Your soul was always meant to be shared. Your life has more meaning when intricately woven with those around you. Sweet friends are a gift; you already know this to be true.

Even so, I always intended for you to know me as fully as I know you. The fellowship of my Spirit is without restraint or boundaries. There's no bad time to call on me, and there are no limitations that you could test. You always have unhindered access to me. Beloved, it is my plan that you find perfect fellowship with me along with sweet, refreshing communion with your friends. Let each reflect the other in joy, comfort, and strength. Just as it is in my heavenly realm, may your relationships be a living testimony of my presence in your life.

Sweet friendships refresh the soul and awaken our hearts with joy,
for good friends are like the anointing oil
that yields the fragrant incense *of God's presence.*

PROVERBS 27:9

Fill up on my love.

Beloved daughter, have you forgotten how much I adore you? You don't have to work harder to receive my love; I offer it freely. My reality supersedes your own. You don't need to keep begging for visions of more, for you have all that I am before you at this very moment. Rest in my goodness today and find the nourishment that keeps your soul thriving, even in the harshest of climates. Winds will not break but bend you, and you will find yourself closer to my perspective. You have not lost anything that will not return more bountiful, beautiful, and full.

I promise that what is coming is more glorious than you can imagine. Your life in mine is only just beginning. You are growing up in my love and partnering with my mercy work that has already filled your life. Use your agency and the power and authority I have given you, daughter. Fly into the great unknown with my Sprit-Wind as your guide and my love as your sustenance.

Fasten your hearts to the love of God
and receive the mercy of our Lord Jesus Christ,
who gives us eternal life.

JUDE 1:21

March

You are gifted with more.

Wake up, my darling, and see what I am already doing in and around you. There is a stream that flows from the river Life, and it's running right through your heart. It never runs dry. Drink deeply today of my measureless kindness. It will fill and refresh you. Your strength will return with my love as your sustenance. Where you have felt depleted, you will overflow again.

You will see me in the light reflecting from your eyes. There is more to see, more to be, and more to do—and it's all good. Will you trust me to guide you into goodness as you awaken to life once more? Look and see, daughter. I am all around. I have not abandoned you for a moment. Do not give up hope, for there's no room for despair when you feast on my glory. Eat, drink, and delight in my abundant goodness. There's no need to ration my love, daughter. There is always more.

Listen! Are you thirsty for more?
Come to the refreshing waters and drink.
Even if you have no money,
come, buy, and eat.
Yes, come and buy all the wine and milk you desire—
it won't cost a thing.

ISAIAH 55:1

I never stop.

I pursue you with my burning presence all the days of your life. At times, it is all-consuming, while in other moments it is a persistent flame that lights the path in front of you. I promise that I will never abandon the work that I began. I never stop restoring what is broken and working wonders in the midst of adversity.

Lift up your gaze to mine; look and see the resolution in my eyes. My affection for you is unmatched, and my delight does not waver for even a moment. I am your good and faithful Father, your Advocate, and your deliverer. Let me be your confidence, for I am as faithful as the sunrise, I am consistent in kindness, and I am persistent in mercy. Even my correction is full of grace that lifts you up rather than of shame that pushes you away. Look around and see what I am doing. Lean into my voice, and I will share with you the wisdom that reveals treasures hidden in darkness. Trust in my faithfulness, and you will never be disappointed!

You have always been, and always will be, my King.
You are the mighty conqueror,
working wonders all over the world.

PSALM 74:12

I restore your strength.

Lean into my power, love, as I cover you with my mercy. Why do you rely on your own capacity when I offer you my limitless strength for your weakness? There's no need to strive, child, for I restore you in rest. I strengthen you in my powerful love with the saturation of my presence. My kindness reestablishes the hope of my unfailing faithfulness toward you within the landscape of your heart.

Take courage in my glorious grace. You are mine, and I am weaving the thread of my redemption through the fabric of your life. There will be no area left untouched by revival. I protect the humble ones, and I lift up those whom life has beaten down. Simply trust in me, and you will find the confidence and serenity that keeps your heart in perfect peace. You are living in my life-giving light, and no detail goes unnoticed. In my life, you can find abundance to quench every thirst and alleviate every need. Drink deeply today and be filled with my power.

> He was so kind, so gracious to me.
> Because of his passion toward me,
> he made everything right and he restored me.
>
> PSALM 116:5

You are covered by kindness.

Y ou are living under the canopy of my kindness. If you ran as far as you could, you would never reach the edges, for it is greater than your limitations. You cannot escape the force of my mercy, no matter how hard you try. My covenant of compassion and love covers you; it is a vow that cannot be broken.

See how I have wrapped you up in my great grace. I have swaddled you with my loving-kindness. I will lead you in the pathways of my peace all the days of your life. Look to me, child, at every turn. I am smoothing out the path in front of you so that you know where to walk.

There is no danger of depleting my vast resources of affection—let me revive your hope in my love again today. I never turn a deaf ear to my dear ones. Rest assured that I hear every cry of your heart, even the ones you've forgotten about. Find your joy today in my delight, for I love you more than you can imagine!

Lord, how wonderfully you bless the righteous.
Your favor wraps around each one and covers them
under your canopy of kindness and joy.

PSALM 5:12

Follow the path of healing.

As I lead you along the pathway of peace, you will find restoration for your brokenness and healing for every wound. I am full of resurrection power. Do you realize that the same Spirit that raised Christ from the grave is alive in you? You have not reached the end of my kindness over your life. What I have done before I will do again, and even more.

What I promised the apostles through Jesus is your inheritance. Look at the wonders that Jesus offered in his lifetime. Look at all of the miracles! And yet, be assured—now is the time for even greater things. Christ declared that through the Spirit at work within you, you will do even more than he accomplished. As he healed, so you will heal. As he led people into eternal freedom, so will you point others toward my everlasting kindness. Follow the path that has been set out before you in accordance with my kingdom ways. When you experience freedom, set others free. When you are healed, release healing to others. You are equipped, and the power of my love will meet you at every juncture.

As you keep walking forward on God's paths
all your stumbling ways will be divinely healed!

HEBREWS 12:13

I make you new.

Darling, you are so dear to my heart. What a beautiful testimony of growth your life is. Look back with me and see how far you have come. My loyal love has led you down the path of renewal that has made all things new in your life. And I'm not finished with you yet.

Take heart today and know that I am your faithful Father who works all things together for your benefit. Let the cleansing flow of my compassion cover every doubt and every fear. Look through the lens of my mercy, for there is no disappointment here. Where you see failure, I see a new opportunity to offer my redemption power. Nothing in your life remains untouched by my restorative love. I envelop you with the power of my Spirit. Open up and receive the newness I am offering you even now. What feels stale will be refreshed in me. You can be confident that my work in your life is good, daughter. Lean into my perspective today, and you will be rejuvenated by what you see.

If anyone is enfolded into Christ, he has become an entirely new creation. All that is related to the old order has vanished. Behold, everything is fresh and new.

2 CORINTHIANS 5:17

Release a fresh sound.

A s a new day has dawned, so is there a completely clean slate before you. Take a moment and breathe in the present, where you and I are one. As your lungs fill with fresh air, let your mind meditate on my nearness. I am with you right here and now, as close as I've ever been. Nothing can separate you from my love, nor can anything keep me away from your heart.

There's no need to rush into action, and there's no pressure to perform. Simply be still and know that I am God. Let your mind, your heart, and your body become aware of my greatness and my goodness over your life. As your heart fills to overflow with my affection, respond as you will. Let the rhythm of your dancing feet be a cadence of praise; let the timbre of your voice echo the refrain of your heart. Whether with loud abandon or soft and tender melodies, release what is building inside of you. Freely express with your whole being who you are and who I've created you to be. Come alive, dear one. This is what brings me glory, for your freedom is my delight.

Compose new melodies that release new praises to the Lord.
Play his praises on instruments
with the anointing and skill he gives you.

PSALM 33:3

You are blooming.

As the spring rains shower the earth and feed the seeds hidden in the soil, so has my love been washing over you. The winter is over, love. As the sun rises over your being, new life is springing up. The barrenness of cold days has drawn to an end. A new season of growth and beauty is at hand. Let your eyes open to the signs around you.

What you thought was your end was an opportunity for seeds of new life to take root in the death of old dreams. Redemption is here. As you have rested, I have been tending to the vulnerable places of your heart. You will see a rich harvest bloom from the garden of your heart that we pruned and tended. I know you had trouble seeing how anything good would come of the shearing process. And yet the fruit of your surrender will taste sweeter than anything you've experienced up until now. Your faithfulness to trust, even in the uncertainty, will be made clear now in the sweet taste of resurrection. I always bring beauty out of the ashes of destruction. Look and see, beloved, how much you have grown. Your life is releasing the sweet fragrance of a bud in bloom.

The budding vines of new life
are now blooming everywhere.
The fragrance of their flowers whispers,
"There is change in the air."

SONG OF SONGS 2:13

Live in my power.

My beloved, I have equipped you with everything you need for an abundant Spirit life. I have rested my power on you through my presence. Take courage, for you do not rely on your own strength. My resources of grave-robbing power are accessible to you whenever you need it. Exercise your faith and test out my mercy. It will never let you down.

You follow the law of my love when you align yourself with my mercy. Be empowered by my grace to live an overcoming life, full of my kindness and my restorative nature. The letter of the law that requires perfection does not bind you. I have already perfected you in the blood of my holy and spotless Son. There is nothing left to do. You have no distance left to cover. You live in the freedom of my deliverance, so live it well. Be free. Offer the same freedom to others and point them to me with acts of outlandish kindness toward them. Pray for the sick, forgive those who wrong you, and offer compassion to those whom others overlook. This is the kind of life that my Spirit empowers.

Now that we have been fully released from the power of the law, we are dead to what once controlled us. ... We may serve God by living in the freshness of a new life in the power of the Holy Spirit.

ROMANS 7:6

We are in this together.

There's no need to rely on your own knowledge and strength to face this day. You have only to call out to me, and I will answer. I have not left you on your own to figure out how to get through. I answer each one of your cries with my help. Take my hand and let me lead you into my glory as I fuel your spirit with my liquid love. Even in the unknown, you have my peace as your portion.

You have no need to fear when my security is your foundation. Don't let anxiety overtake you, for you are not alone. Let my presence be your comfort as you journey through this life. I promise that you will not waste away in isolation. My living Word will be your sustenance, and my wraparound presence will be your covering. Let your heart receive the revelation of my nearness as I draw even closer to you. Don't hesitate to call on me whenever you need a fresh reminder of my favor. My Spirit is with you; you cannot wander outside of my awareness. Here I am with you, no matter what comes. Lean into my love every step of the way.

Now you are ready, my bride, to come with me as we climb the highest peaks together. Come with me through the archway of trust.

Song of Songs 4:8

I offer you strength.

Child, do not hesitate to come to me in your weakness. Though you are vulnerable, I will cover you and infuse you with strength straight from my mighty mercy. I never turn away the defenseless. I surround you with the power of my unrelenting love. There's no need to despair at your own helplessness, for I always more than make up for it. Why rely on your own resources when you have my abundance to reinforce you?

Come alive in my living waters, for there is nothing that can keep you from being lifted by the weight of my great affection. Just lean back and let me raise you up. This is a time for radical trust in my faithfulness. Just as I parted the waters for the Israelites so that they could walk on the dry riverbed to freedom, so will I keep leading you into liberty. Let my grace empower your frail efforts; you will be astounded at the miracle of my great power in your life as you step out in faith.

Yahweh is the *one and only* everlasting God,
the Creator of all you can see and imagine.
He never gets weary or worn out. ...
He empowers the feeble
and infuses the powerless with increasing strength.

Isaiah 40:28, 29

I am holding you.

I have drawn you close to my heart and embraced you with my affection. Lean in, beloved, and let your heart settle and sync to the rhythm of my own. You've already been living by its beat. My heart is full of love for your taking. Breathe in, daughter, and let your lungs fill with the hope of my nearness. There is safety here in my embrace. I will keep you secure, covered in my kindness.

You will find your healing right here as you allow me to hold you. Rest in my presence that enfolds you. I will restore everything that has been taken, and it will be better than you can imagine. For every loss, I will give you treasure from my own storehouse. Let me wrap you up in my love that makes all things new. You don't have to figure anything out right now, daughter. Simply let go and let me shelter you in my wraparound presence. I will keep you in perfect peace as you press into my thoughts for you. My love knows no bounds. It lifts you up whenever life beats you down, and it meets you wherever you are. Be still and be held.

Protect me from harm; keep an eye on me like you would a child reflected in the twinkling of your eye. Yes, hide me within the shelter of your embrace, under your outstretched wings.

PSALM 17:8

Renewal is here.

Today be baptized afresh in the living waters of my loving affection. Submerge yourself in the sheltering embrace of my presence as I wrap around you with my delight. Now is the time to rise up again, beloved, for I am doing a new thing. The barrenness of winter has come to an end. Do you see the signs of new life springing up around you? It is here; it is time.

Let the joy of a new season fill your heart as you recognize the life that is growing inside of you. The seeds sown in previous seasons now sprout to life in the light of my mercy. It is a time of celebration as you cultivate what breaks through the surface. When you thought you had reached the end of your story, I spoke redemption over you. Now do you see it? Now do you understand that what falls to the earth in its dying breaks through the ground when it is ready with resurrection power as its fuel? Renewal is built into the rhythm of creation, and you are no exception. Rejoice, for new life is budding before your very eyes.

As the snow and rain that fall from heaven
do not return until they have accomplished their purpose,
soaking the earth and causing it to sprout with new life.

ISAIAH 55:10

You are safe here.

I reside in the peace and quiet of your soul. You don't have to dig deep to find it. Let my breath of peace awaken your senses as you draw near. Come closer, love, and walk directly into my compassionate kindness. Here is the rest you have been looking for, right here in my presence. Let the chaos of this world fade into the background as you find me now in this present moment.

I keep you safe in the embrace of my loving kindness. My goodness wraps around you even if you struggle to see it right now. You can trust me to keep watch over your heart in the good days and through the difficult ones. There is no difference in my attention, love. I am here, and I am for you. Find your home in the shelter of my affection. It is your sustenance, your strength, and your resting place. Right now, beloved, lean back into my arms and rest. You can trust that no matter what the day brings, I have my firm grip of grace on your life. I will keep you for as long as the present is called *today*.

You will sleep like a baby, safe and sound—
your rest will be sweet and secure.
You will not be subject to terror, for it will not terrify you.

PROVERBS 3:24–25

Refreshing streams of life.

Are you tired and overloaded by the worries of this world? I welcome you into my living presence that refreshes your soul. Come rest by the streams of living water and be filled by the fruit of my Word. I am not requiring you to do more in this moment. I meet you in every turn of your attention. My splendor shines on you right where you are. Like a flower turning to the sun, look to me. I am the source of life itself, and I will revive your waning heart.

Look at the areas where you thought all hope was lost only to have found that my redemption breathed life into fallen hopes and brought you into something new. You have seen me work things out for you before, and I haven't stopped being faithful. What you see as a dead end I am making into a garden of possibility and joy. Nothing is impossible for me, beloved. Be refreshed in my Spirit today and find that hope is still alive.

I will open up refreshing streams on the barren hills
and springing fountains in the valleys.
I will make the desert a pleasant pool
and the dry land springs of water.

ISAIAH 41:18

My promises are sure.

My beloved, my covenant vow with you will never be broken. What I decree, I do. What I foretell, I follow through on. Let my merciful faithfulness carry you through the hard days, and lean into the current of my grace. You cannot prevent the fulfillment of my promises. So take heart, for I cannot be deterred from my mercy. Your weakness makes my power perfect.

Let your soul find its strength in my devotion. I am more reliable than the rising of the sun in the east. My kindness is more consistent than the rotation of the earth on its axis. You are full of my glory, as is all of creation. If you cannot see me in yourself, let me give you the lens of my redemption that offers clear vision of the deposits of my compassionate character. You will find that there is more to you that reflects of my kindness than not. And what is not in alignment is an opportunity for further growth. Exercise your faith today by clinging to my Word in and over your life. Declare my life over the lives of those around you. My intentions are full of mercy, and they always will be.

The Lord Yahweh, Commander of Angel Armies,
makes this solemn decree:
"Be sure of this: Just as I have planned, so it will be.
Every purpose of my heart will surely come to pass."

Isaiah 14:24

My power changes you.

Let the washing of my Word flow through your heart and mind today as you press into my perfect presence. I am the bearer of good news, and you are the recipient of my great grace. Let me remind you if you've forgotten. I have broken every chain of shame and the sin that entangled you. You are free in the lifeblood of Jesus, who sacrificed his life so that all could freely live in communion with me. Come closer and let my love fill your heart with the knowledge of marvelous mercy that always reaches you.

You are living in the power of redemption and resurrection. The old is gone, and the new has come. You have experienced the power of my grace that has made the coping mechanisms that once served you lose their luster. My kingdom's ways are your sustenance and your wisdom. You have more than you will ever need in the resources of my Spirit life in you. The fruit of your life, when aligned with my love, is sweeter than the sweetest honeycomb. My grace is carrying you, so be encouraged.

This is the wonderful message that is being spread everywhere, powerfully changing hearts throughout the earth, just like it has changed you! Every believer of this good news bears the fruit of eternal life as they experience the reality of God's grace.

COLOSSIANS 1:6

This is not the end.

B eloved one, do not be discouraged by the testing of your hope while wading through the brush of uncertainty. I am with you, and I see the way clearly. You can trust me to continue to guide you with my perfect vision, so take hold of my hand. Though you cannot see where we could possibly go from here, I know precisely where to lead you.

Breathe deeply of my loyal love today as I flood your mind with my perfect peace. Even in uncertainty, your heart can know the constancy of assurance that my goodness sustains you. My resurrection power already works in your life. I make all things new, child, and I won't ever stop. Root your faith deeply in my affection, and your soul will always know the abundance of my kingdom's fruit. Even here, your capacity for wisdom and understanding grows. The eyes of your heart are being enlightened to see from my higher perspective. There's no need to fear when I am leading you in love. And love, I am leading you.

You bring me a continual revelation of resurrection life,
the path to the bliss that brings me face-to-face with you.
PSALM 16:11

I surround you with comfort.

My dearly loved child, let me wrap around you with the presence of my living love today. I am your very present comfort, never leaving you to drown in your pain. My heart is full of gentle kindness, and it is yours. Let me refresh you with my peace that eases the heaviness of your sorrow. I am the lifter of your head and your strong shelter in every turbulent time.

Let me tend to your broken heart today. You do not have to be strong right now, so there is no use pretending that you're at your best. Melt back into my loving embrace and let my perfect peace surround you. My peace can give you comfort even when the heartache still stings. My presence is a salve to your wounds, and it always offers the abundance of my kingdom. Do not prolong your suffering by denying the comfort that I so freely offer. Let me love you right where you are today. I don't require anything in exchange.

He is the Father of tender mercy and the God of endless comfort.
He always comes alongside us to comfort us in every suffering
so that we can come alongside those who are in any painful trial.

2 CORINTHIANS 1:3–4

Winds of refreshing are blowing.

B eloved, can you feel my Spirit-Wind blowing over your life today? Can you sense my nearness as you go about your day? I am closer than your breath, and yet I am working all over the world. I am not out of touch with you and those you love. Trust that the reality of my ways is strong enough to encompass everything all at once.

Give yourself to the shift that is upon you. Be refreshed in the living waters of my love. Let the replenishing pool of my redemption power revive whatever has grown stale. New life blooms. As birdsong indicates the coming of brighter days, so does my refreshing wind indicate a time of renewal throughout all of nature. Join with creation in celebration as the barren days of winter draw to a close. Just as nature makes room for the regeneration of life, you must do the same. Clear out the brush of old things and prepare for the fruitful season ahead. The time has come for you to enter in with joy!

When you release your Spirit-Wind, life is created, ready to replenish life upon the earth. May God's glorious splendor endure forever!

PSALM 104:30–31

Look up, child.

Look to me today, beloved. Whatever you are facing is not bigger than my unfailing love. Let me surround you with the peace of my presence as you turn your attention toward me. I will never neglect the needs of my beloved ones. My attentive gaze is on you, and I am already working out my mercy power in your life.

You can keep putting your trust in me, for I have not finished working my faithful miracles. Where discouragement keeps your attention on the problem, let your eyes dare look for me, the author of your faith. I am your reliable help in every trouble. My dear, nothing is too trivial for me. What burdens your heart matters to me. Share your heart with me as I remind you how capable I am to lift every weight. I have not grown tired of pouring my mercy over your life, and I have not grown weary of saving you or of redeeming that which seems too far gone. It is impossible to exhaust my love. Look into my eyes and let your heart settle as you realize that I am full of confident kindness, and I am not worried.

May everyone who knows your mercy keep putting their trust in you, for they can count on you for help no matter what. O Lord, you will never, no never, neglect those who come to you.

PSALM 9:10

I am holding fast.

Daughter, I am holding you with a strong grip that won't let go. My loyal love embraces your life with a firm grasp, without the chance of you slipping away. Do not give over to the fear that threatens to cripple you. I am closer than you realize, and I always will be. Your awareness does not affect my nearness, child, but it does influence your own faith. Look and you will find that I am faithful and have never left.

There is no danger of my purposes being lost to the powers of this world. I am victorious. Do you need a reminder of how it is that I work? In my mercy, I lead my lovers out of captivity into freedom. In compassion, I advocate for the weak and defend the vulnerable. In delight, I give beauty for ashes and joy for mourning. In power, I offer strength to those who lean on me. Be refreshed in my living love today, for I am holding you fast in my goodness. My kindness covers you. Keep looking to me so that your heart can find its steady confidence in my faithfulness. I have got you.

Do not yield to fear, for I am always near. Never turn your gaze from me, for I am your *faithful* God. I will infuse you with my strength and help you in every situation. I will hold you firmly with my victorious right hand.

Isaiah 41:10

There is no greater power.

As you live your life aligned with my kingdom through the surrender of your own will and ways, you will find that the fruit of freedom is more expansive than you ever could have imagined. The sweetness of living awakened to the marvelous mercy that covers every piece of your story is more satisfying than striving toward and accomplishing a thousand self-serving goals. I even take your every failure and produce goodness through it.

There's no need to rely on your own limited resources when you have access to my resurrection power. I take what seems hopeless to most and work my redemption power. I will use everything for the benefit of my beloved ones. Watch as I turn even your darkest day into a beaming beacon of my glorious light. You will see the treasures that resulted from the pressures that threatened to smother you. But they didn't. I wouldn't let them. So come and exchange your weakness for my great strength and delight. Arise in the power of my love today. Awaken to life again.

I pray that you will continually experience the immeasurable greatness of God's power made available to you through faith. Then your lives will be an advertisement of this immense power as it works through you!

EPHESIANS 1:19

I am releasing rest.

Daughter, are you tired? Bring me the heavy load of expectations that you carry. Come to me with your weariness, and I will give you restorative rest. There is no need to perform for me; just lie back into my lavish love and let it soak into your soul like a healing salve. This moment is ours, love. Put aside the to-do list and let me fill you with the strength of my joy as you let go of the tension of never-enough.

Child, I have everything you need, so there's no need to keep striving. My load is easy, and it is light, so let's trade. Let me offer you my help. I do all the heavy lifting, so there's no need to bear the burden anymore. You already live in the grace of my favor. Don't keep picking up the responsibility of problems that are not yours to bear. Embrace the freedom I offer you. I promise there will never come a day where my joy and peace are not your perfect portion. Take hold of my rest and let go of everything else, even in the midst of your busyness.

God has offered to us the same promise of entering
into his realm of resting in confident faith.

HEBREWS 4:1

I have got you.

Beloved, the perfect peace of my presence safely surrounds you. Nothing can come against you that will succeed in taking you outside of the realm of my loving kindness. I tend to every detail in your life and tie up every loose end. Nothing slips my notice, so don't worry. I see it all. Press into the courage of confident faith that chooses trust over fear.

Look over your history with me and let me reveal the deposits of my kindness within your story. The depths of my goodness are very present in your life. If you are having trouble seeing yourself from my perspective, look for the unexpected joys and relieved worries in your life. I am always at work in you. Here, now, in this moment, let me love you to life again in my powerful presence. Let my tranquility quiet the storms of your mind. Peace, be still and know that I am with you. I am for you. I am your God, and I am taking care of you both now and forevermore.

Don't worry. For your Father cares deeply
about even the smallest detail of your life.
MATTHEW 10:30–31

Take courage.

I am the author of your story, and I have not lost sight of the plot. Don't fret about whether I will come through for you or not. Wait for me to break through, for it is coming. I will never leave you to fight for yourself. I am your Defender and your strong help in times of trouble. Let my delight over you strengthen your resolve to stand firm in the faith. You can trust my timing and my intentions over your life. Cling to me, and do not forget what I have promised you. I have not swayed from my purposes.

You are the object of my kindness. Let the joy of pure affection flood your senses as you place all your bets on my faithfulness. Take courage, beloved, for I am with you. Soak in the profound peace of my presence, and you will once again feel the firm foundation of my unchanging character underneath your feet. I am not slow to answer; I am already working in the details. Wait for me to move. I'm on the way to burst through the trials before you with my mighty power. I am making a way for you even now.

Cheer up! Take courage all you who love him.
Wait for him to break through for you, all who trust in him!
PSALM 31:24

I won't let you fall.

Beloved one, my firm grip of grace holds you steady. I will never let go. My tender affection is undeterred by the shaking going on around you. Nothing can damage my view of you, daughter. I say it again: nothing can weaken my love. No failure, no desperate attempts at control, no attacks of my own character—nothing can undermine the kindness of my heart toward you. You cannot talk me out of my affection and neither can anyone else.

Lean back into my arms. When everything around you is unsteady, I hold you firm in my safe embrace. Are you beginning to understand the reach of my love? You can always trust me, even when your heart struggles to understand. I don't tire of teaching you my ways. And even if you choose not to believe me, I still won't relent in tenderness toward you. I have given you a lifetime of todays, and I am pouring my never-ending stream of mercy over your life. Don't fear when testing comes, for I never change.

Now I live with the confidence that there is nothing in the universe with the power to separate us from God's love. … There is nothing in our present or future circumstances that can weaken his love.

ROMANS 8:38

My mercy knows no bounds.

I lead you into the abounding kindness of my heart every time you pursue my presence. I reveal the mercy that is at work in your life, right under your nose. I am with you, child. I am for you. I hear your constant cry for restoration of relationships and of health, and I am working it out. What a reflection of my own compassionate heart is that request. My goodness guides you, daughter.

The refining power of Christ's blood washed you clean. My presence is the assurance of my great love that pursues you every day of your life. Every moment is a new opportunity to grab hold of my marvelous mercy. It is always new, always fresh, always relevant. Lean into my lavish love and find your soul refreshed in its living waters. Drink deeply of my delight as you press in to know my heart. Let my kindness be the reservoir of resources that you draw from as you go about your day. I am with you—so very close, beloved.

I will tell again of the faithful, gracious acts of Yahweh and praise him for everything he has done for us—the wonderful goodness, the riches of his mercy, which he has shown to the house of Israel, and the abundance of his endless love.

ISAIAH 63:7

You are my beloved.

Y ou cannot exaggerate my tender love for you. There is no beginning and no end to my affection. It fills the universe and still keeps on going. My kindness is strong enough to cover every misstep and lift you out of the drudgery of the cycles of shame. If you don't believe but one thing today, let it be that my mercy pursues you. There is no length I wouldn't go to save you, so let the light of my delight fill your heart now. Put down your resistance. Lay aside your excuses. You cannot talk me out of my love!

Beloved, come close and listen to my heartbeat. Its rhythm is steady and sure; it never falters. Let me answer your questions about your identity. Bring me your doubts and fears. Let me show you the truth in my unwavering affection toward you. If it doesn't feel too good to be true, you haven't grasped it quite yet. Go deeper, love, and do not be dissuaded by lies that tell you you're not worthy of being my child. You are mine, and that is enough. Come into the fullness of your inheritance as my own and don't settle for anything less.

The same way a loving father feels toward his children—
that's but a sample of your tender feelings toward us,
your beloved children, who live in awe of you.

PSALM 103:13

Arise and shine.

As you soak in the atmosphere of my presence, my glory shines on you. You are full of light, my child, and it is getting brighter with every turn of your attention toward the eternal within you. Today is the day to rise up with the light of my constant compassion shining from your life. When you align your days with my law of love, reaching out in consistent kindness to those around you, there is no question that you belong to me.

Today find your holy hope in my extravagant affection. Let me hold the heavy things of this life. I will work it all out for your benefit. I never fail to follow through on my promises, and I never will. You just live as I call you to and as I have shown you. Let mercy guard your heart. Reach out just as my love always reaches out by never holding back kindness laced with humility. You have everything you need today; you are fully loved. Now arise in that love and let it shine unhindered in your life!

Don't hide your light! Let it shine brightly before others, so that the commendable things you do will shine as light upon them, and then they will give their praise to your Father in heaven.

MATTHEW 5:16

I don't give up.

Let me lead you deeper into the light of my love today. My faithful kindness is your plentiful portion. Take my hand and trust that I already know where I am leading you. I do not guide you into suffering but into goodness. And even when you suffer, I am there, working the miracle of my refining power that inspires encouragement from ashes of disappointment. There's no need to fear with me as your Good Shepherd. I will not let you wander beyond my grip of grace.

If the earth gives way beneath your feet, my perfect peace will still be your foundation. There are no surprises to me, and nothing can throw off my intentions for you. Let the liberty of love be your rising song, as it is for all of my people. You are free in me, and you always will be. My compassion chases you down all the days of your life. My kindness covers you wherever you go. There is no step you could take where I am not. My Spirit is your life-strength. Just as I will never give up on you, I give you the strength to keep going. Lean in, love, to my powerful presence. Here is all you need.

"Even if the mountains were to crumble and the hills disappear, my heart of steadfast, faithful love will never leave you, and my covenant of peace with you will never be shaken," says Yahweh, whose love and compassion will never give up on you.

ISAIAH 54:10

April

You are liberated.

C hild, you are free in me. The blood of Christ broke every chain that held you back. The power of sin and death have been broken, and you stand liberated in the light of my everlasting life. In what areas have you felt stuck? Partner with my truth that says you are free indeed. Enter into the light of my truth and find that the lies melt away in the power of my presence. Let my affection draw you into my heart once again.

Nothing can ever separate you from my extravagant loving-kindness. I do not waste it when I direct it toward you. Throw off all the lies that hinder you and come running right into it. Defy the doubt by letting me speak the truth of your identity over you. Let me remind you who I created you to be, my liberated love. You are free to choose as you will, but be sure that in your choosing you never enslave yourself to another. Why would you choose to lock yourself in when I have broken open every prison door? Walk into my freedom today!

The "law" of the Spirit of life flowing through the anointing of Jesus has liberated us from the "law" of sin and death.

ROMANS 8:2

Increase is yours.

Let your heart expand as I speak my words of affectionate truth over your life. There is increase coming to you, so store up my goodness by being full of gratitude. When you recognize and take note of what I have already done and am doing in your life, you add to the storehouse of my compassion within you. Keep an account of my mercies, and you will never doubt that I am for you!

Even now, there is more coming to you. The work I started in you, I am continuing. Partner with me, and you will find that growth quickens in your life. I have been preparing you for harvest, and it is coming, child. The long days of winter had their purpose, and now you will experience the increase that comes in restoration of life. Where it seemed as if everything was being stripped away, your roots were growing deep under the surface. Can you feel the greater expanse of my kingdom within you? A new day has dawned, and it is full of my abundant love that will cause a surge in the returns for your labor. Is your heart ready for more?

> Increase is coming, so enlarge your tent
> and add extensions to your dwelling.
> Hold nothing back! Make the tent ropes longer
> and the pegs stronger.
>
> ISAIAH 54:2

APRIL 3

Be bold.

My love is a never-ending stream of sustenance for your soul. You can find everything you need in the life-blood of my unending kindness. My perfect peace holds you steady in the fiercest storms, and it gives you clarity to see my goodness at work. Yield to my heart today. Don't fight the current of my mercy, for it is the strength that will keep you on the pathway of surrendered love.

Do you doubt the power of my life in yours? Take confidence in my Word and walk out the ways of peace that I have prepared for you. If ever you need a reminder of what living love looks like, study the life of Jesus. His example is not unattainable for you because you are a dearly loved child of the living God. You have alive in you the same Spirit who raised Christ from the dead. You have unhindered access to connection with me at all times. Do not hesitate to call on me, for you were never meant to live in your own strength. I have empowered you with my Spirit, so take courage and be bold in my love.

Surrender to God. Stand up to the devil and resist him
and he will turn and run away from you.

JAMES 4:7

I am the resurrection.

Behold, I am the resurrection and the life. All who look to me will find their hopes fulfilled and their deep desires satisfied. In the landscape of my kingdom, an abundance of joy exists, tethered to the peace of my persistent presence. I am alive, and that is reason enough to celebrate, for in my life, all will find their purpose.

No one who looks to the Lamb will be left untouched by the drenching love of mercy's movement. See how my hands bear the scars of all-surrendering love. See how my side was pierced though I was pure. On my head, where there was a crown of thorns made to mock me, now a glorious crown of righteous authority rests in its place. I am the way, the truth, and the life. Come to me, and you have full access to the Father of love. Come boldly, with a surrendered heart and let your soul be resurrected to life in my presence!

"Martha," Jesus said, "You don't have to wait until then.
I am the Resurrection, and I am Life Eternal.
Anyone who clings to me in faith, even though he dies,
will live forever."

JOHN 11:25

Be filled with my good news.

Beloved, feast on my truth and refuse to gorge on the bad reports of the day. You do not belong to a kingdom of this world, which dictates that you must respond to tragedy with despair. Hopelessness is a liar, and it leaves my resurrection power out of the picture. You belong to my heavenly kingdom where every wrong is made right, the sick receive healing, bodies rise from the dead, and peace prevails. That is good news!

I am not asking you to ignore what is happening around you. Rather I am beckoning you to rise above it. It is not the final page, and your response gets to be a part of my redemptive story. So join with me. Let hope arise in your heart once again as you give over to my gracious ways. Where you had dug your heels in, now get down and reposition your feet to sprint ahead. I see the future, and it is good, my love—filled with compassionate responses and kindness from those who bear my likeness. Join with my army of lovers as I make all things new once again.

Like a drink of cool water to a weary, thirsty soul,
so hearing good news revives the spirit.
PROVERBS 25:25

Clothe yourself in light.

A new day of destiny dawns over your life. See that as the darkness diminishes, I am right here by your side. I have been here all along. As my glory shines on your life, abandon the old ways of living that don't suit you any longer as a child of the light. I am washing your mind with the living waters of my Spirit. The oil of my presence saturates you with unconditional love.

Remove from your life that which does not align with my complete compassion. Throw off the things that keep snaring, trapping, and enslaving you. Whatever is not done in freedom is an indicator of the old way. But I have made you new. My mercy washes over you with constancy. There is nothing that is exempt from the power of my loyal love and the might of my resurrection. Live as a child of the light, for that is who you are. When you live with honor, who can argue against it? Hold on to loyal love and don't let go.

Night's darkness is dissolving away as a new day of destiny dawns. So we must once and for all strip away what is done in the shadows of darkness, removing it like filthy clothes. And once and for all we clothe ourselves with the radiance of light as our weapon.

ROMANS 13:12

Let there be unity.

Child, listen closely to what I have to say today. I have called you to a life of reconciliation. The thread of my loving mercy weaves through all of creation. It reconciles every disagreement, resolves every tension, and reunites the hearts of those led astray. I have brought you into a kingdom—a family—knitted together by unfailing love. Let your own life reflect the unity of my heart. Don't let petty grievances keep you from extending mercy through forgiveness. There is no better love than the love that lays down its self-protecting armor.

In the same way that I have shown you compassion, offer kindness to others. When you are able, give the benefit of the doubt. Let your holy pursuit of peace lead you to the kind of blessing you find in restorative relationship. You can't help but promote my heart when you point others toward my marvelous mercy. Every one of my children who reunites with my perfect intentions for them is drenched in the same lavish love you are living in. Don't be shy; the world is waiting for a better hope.

God has made all things new, and reconciled us to himself,
and given us the ministry of reconciling others to God.

2 Corinthians 5:18

I'm not finished with you.

Beloved, as long as you are drawing breath, I am at work in your life. You have not reached the end of your story, and there is no danger of you being plucked from my love. Do you forget that I am renowned as the master restorer? I am the God who makes a way for his people in the wilderness and leads them to streams of living water. I have not forgotten what I promised you, so let the eyes of your faith be opened now and allow fresh vision, unencumbered by disappointment, to be restored.

I am continually renewing you. No sufferings or joys in your life will go wasted. Even the darkest nights I will use for my purposes, and the most painful circumstances will produce life. There is so much more at work than you can comprehend in your own ability. Let me give you a higher perspective that opens up your understanding and brings clarity to confusion. Be filled with my kindness, and you will find that possibilities open up before you in unprecedented ways. I am doing my good and faithful work in your life. All you need to do is trust. Let my faithfulness fill you with peace of mind and heart today.

You have acquired new creation life which is continually being renewed into the likeness of the One who created you; giving you the full revelation of God.

COLOSSIANS 3:10

I am not surprised.

L et me encourage you with my all-pervading wisdom today. Nothing within you surprises me. I see you with perfect vision, my beloved. Your choices do not throw me off. There are no mysteries to me. I read your heart like an open book, so there is no need to hide. Dark is as light to me. There is nothing concealed from my merciful understanding. What confuses you is as clear as day to me. Let this be an encouragement to your heart. I completely accept you and cover you with my loving-kindness all the days of your life.

Do you not know my compassionate nature by now? How fervently I love you? No force can compete against my fierce kindness that endlessly pursues you. Why fight its current? Let go and let it carry you straight into my glory-filled presence. Just as I see straight to the heart of every matter, I see you, beloved. Let me love you to life in the stream of my great grace once again.

You are so intimately aware of me, Lord.
You read my heart like an open book
and you know all the words I'm about to speak
before I even start a sentence!
You know every step I will take before my journey even begins.

PSALM 139:3–4

My mercy is strong.

Daughter, my covenant of mercy covers you, and I will never break my vow. Keep putting your trust in me, for I am faithful. Stir up the remembrance of my loyal love over your life when you start to waver. Though nothing can measure the generosity of my heart, can you not recognize its presence in your life? The power of my kindness is unmatched in all of the earth. Though hatred drives people to violence, the passion of my great love is stronger than the most destructive forces that man could conjure. Does not resurrection render powerless the devastation of death? Nothing can escape my redemption.

Set your expectations on the goodness of my kingdom today. Set your hopes on my unfailing character that always follows through in faithfulness. Hitch your faith to my unshakeable mercy that breathes life into dry bones, brings healing to every disease, and leads those who have surrendered to the abundance of my promised forever-kingdom. Be strengthened in hope today, unwavering in confidence that my intentions for you are good.

> Higher than the highest heavens—
> that's how high your tender mercy extends!
> Greater than the grandeur of heaven above
> is the greatness of your loyal love, towering over all
> who fear you and bow down before you!
>
> PSALM 103:11

Give it to me.

Beloved, trust my heart of affection today as I lovingly lead you into surrender. I see what you have been holding on to. Are you ready to release the tight grip you have kept on it? Let me show you a better way. I know that you have suffered, and I see how you have tried to protect yourself. Love, let's take a look at what you have been hiding behind those walls. Can you see that the wound is now infected because of neglect? Do not be ashamed, for I am your healer, and I will tend to your injuries.

Can you see now that holding onto unforgiveness has kept you from letting my loving-kindness mend the tears in your heart? Let me give you the peace of my mercy in exchange for letting go of the resentment that has kept you in turmoil. I will cover you with the abundance of tender love and care that you require to be made whole. I am your healer, your deliverer, and your Defender. So trust my ways as you consider the character of my kindness. I will not let you down.

Why would you hold a grudge in your heart
toward your neighbor who lives right next door?

PROVERBS 3:29

Christ is the source.

The image of my Son fully embodies my living love. Through him all of creation finds its satisfaction. There is a rich heritage of faithfulness accessible to all of my loyal lovers through communion with Emmanuel. I am the God who is with you, a very near presence. The source of life itself fully knows and extravagantly loves you. Throw off your hesitation and find the consummation of pure delight in my vibrant kindness. What do you need today? Find it here in the pool of my great grace.

If you lack anything, you will find the fulfillment of abundance in my Living Word. Lean into the kindness of my heart as you search out wisdom, for highest understanding is found within my marvelous mercy. There is no higher law than love. So look to the teachings of Jesus to guide your steps and you will never waver from my pathway of peace. Walk in the way of living love, and you will discover the treasures of my kingdom planted in your path.

Through the Son everything was created, both in the heavenly realm
and on the earth, all that is seen and all that is unseen. ...
It was all created through him and for his purpose!

COLOSSIANS 1:16

I offer you tender affection.

B eloved, come close now. Don't hesitate to draw near to me with whatever you are carrying today. Does your heart waver with confusion? Does fear burden you? Is the pain of heartbreak tearing you open? Bring it all. I will not offer you a lecture, and I don't want you to pretend that you are ok when you're not. I can handle the reality of you as you are.

Take the cup of my love and drink it up. I offer you comfort for your sorrow and healing salve for your wounds. There is no shortage of compassion in my heart toward you. Don't be fooled into thinking that I only love you when you feel loveable. My tender affection is unwavering toward you, no matter the day or the circumstance. You are always my dear one in whom I delight. Dare to hope that the power of my kindness is enough to sustain you. Let me remind you who I am as you lay down your misconceptions at my feet.

Look at how much encouragement you've found in your relationship with the Anointed One! You are filled to overflowing with his comforting love. You have experienced a deepening friendship with the Holy Spirit and have felt his tender affection and mercy.

PHILIPPIANS 2:1

Hide yourself in my faithfulness.

Run into my heart today and find yourself hidden in my devoted love. My faithfulness is not dependent on your own, dearest. I am always reaching out to you with my unwavering affection. You will find your true home in my presence. Let me show you just what I am doing for you in these days. Let me open your eyes to the unshakeable hope you have in me!

The systems of this world are unreliable and constantly shifting. But I am a firm foundation, and I never stray from my purposes for my people. I am redemption hope, and even more—I am the One who brings life from death in every single situation. My faithful love leaves no circumstance untouched. Be comforted by my nearness and my advocacy for you and yours. I am faithful to every promise that I have set out. I will not abandon you for even a moment. Let your faith find its strength in the ocean of my mercy right here and now. You are woven into my love, and you can trust my leadership!

Now we have run into his heart to hide ourselves in his faithfulness.
This is where we find his strength and comfort, for he empowers us
to seize what has already been established ahead of time—
an unshakeable hope!

HEBREWS 6:18

Follow the breakthrough.

My dearest, look through the lens of my goodness and see what I am doing in your life. Let the passion that once fueled your courageous heart be restored as you realize that I never lifted my presence from you. The dormancy of winter may have convinced you that all development had ground to a halt, but what you couldn't see was that the stripping down was leading to restoration. The seeds that had fallen are now getting ready to break through the surface.

The coming growth exceeds anything you've experienced up until this point. The bounty of the fruit will be sweet and will fill you with the greatest appreciation of life. Look and see where there are signs of spring and follow the breakthrough. See, restoration is at hand. Renewal is here. Fill up on the good news of resurrection life all around you. Let trust be restored as you recognize that I have been tending to you all this time. Get ready for more, child. There is so much goodness coming!

Let my passion for life be restored,
tasting joy in every breakthrough you bring to me.
Hold me close to you with a willing spirit
that obeys whatever you say.

PSALM 51:12

I am a gentle shepherd.

As an attentive shepherd lovingly tends to his flock, so do I gently lead you and keep watch over you. When one of my beloved ones wanders outside of the safety of godly community, I leave the masses and go after the one. Do not fear, for you will never be lost from me. All those who look to me will be satisfied.

Do not despise the kindness of my leadership, and don't be fooled by those who exercise their strength through putting others down. The proud have no authority in my kingdom. Instead I will lift up the humble lovers. Follow those who lead in my likeness. Those who offer mercy rather than condemnation, grace instead of harsh judgments. My character cannot be changed. If you want to know where my judgments land, look at what the Scriptures say. I do not harshly judge the weak and helpless. Rather it is those who think they know better that will find themselves without mercy, for they have not extended any. But now, child, trust my affection and its power to heal and revive your weary soul. I gather you close in my welcoming embrace. Let me love you to life once again.

He will care for you as a shepherd tends his flock, gathering the weak lambs and taking them in his arms. He carries them close to his heart and gently leads those that have young.

ISAIAH 40:11

I am proud of you.

Dearest daughter, how can I convey how deeply I delight in you? When you press into my love, you will find that there is nothing that you could ever do to convince me in or out of my love. I see the difficult choices you have made and the ways in which you've aligned your life with my Word. I've taken note of every moment of surrender and each thought you have taken captive. What a wonderful warrior you are!

You have not disappointed me, my love. You cannot surprise me. Even in your deepest sorrow and greatest letdown, your identity as my child never comes into question. You cannot venture out of my great affection for you, and you cannot wander from the grip of my grace. You are firmly found in me. Lay down your self-disenchantment today and let me fill you with the wonders of my love again. My joy over your life is unparalleled. You cannot imagine the deep delight of my heart that encompasses your being. From the moment I imagined you until now, I have never wavered in my tenderness toward you. Let me reawaken your heart to life in the light of my love.

When a father observes his child living in godliness,
he is ecstatic with joy—nothing makes him prouder!
PROVERBS 23:24

The dark night is ending.

B eloved, I am shining on you right now in this moment. I am breaking through the clouds of confusion so that the rays of my wisdom can burn off the fog of doubt. Can you see it, love? Can you see the way the landscape of your heart is coming into focus once again? Come alive in my love. It's time to dance in the dawn of my delight, for the morning has come. The long, dark night is done.

Wake up, dear daughter, and see that everything that was hidden in the shadows of night is now clearly visible. The pieces of you that you thought you had lost along the way are at hand. Open your eyes and let me show you. Dreams long forgotten are being stirred up once again. Feast on my mercy as I reveal the life within you. More is available to you than you can realize. Take my hand and let me lead you into joy today as you rediscover the treasures of my goodness within you. The light of life is shining on you.

Let the sunrise of your love end our dark night.
Break through our clouded dawn again!
Only you can satisfy our hearts,
filling us with songs of joy to the end of our days.

PSALM 90:14

Hold on to loyal love.

There are many competing bids for your attention in these days, my daughter. There is no lack of opportunity to grow and change in a myriad of ways. Remember that I never call you to strive in growth. Just as a child who grows up in a safe and loving family develops with the freedom of joy and delight, so are you surrounded by the affection of my heart that fosters healthy growth, whether you give it attention or not. Become like a child in the way you approach the growth of your faith: test things out, listen to my loving correction, rest when you're spent, and play for delight's sake.

Above all, no matter what you do or don't do, hold on to loyal love and don't loosen your grip. Be confident of my reliable kindness that never leaves you. My compassion covers you, and my goodness overwhelmingly fills your life. Continue to align your values with my kingdom ways and you will never end up in the company of the foolish. You will live in the freedom of honor and integrity with my words of life as your guide.

Hold on to loyal love and don't let go,
and be faithful to all that you've been taught.
Let your life be shaped by integrity,
with truth written upon your heart.
PROVERBS 3:3

Let your song rise.

Today let the song of your heart rise to your lips. Sing out the melody of praise that dwells within the spirit-center of your being. I don't desire a scripted love song when a spontaneous refrain waits to escape your mouth. All of heaven listens as you offer your adoration. It is a beautiful thing to behold, your response to my faithful love in your life.

I hear the symphonies of your heart adding to the soundtrack of your praise. What a beautiful offering it is. I never tire of hearing your voice. But when you take a break, lean in and hear the song I am singing over you. What a call and response we have going. Beloved, can you sense my wraparound presence that enfolds you in my loving embrace? The light of my goodness is all around you. As you profess your faith through song, can you not feel the weighty exchange happening? As you lift your praise, I rain down the refreshing waters of my delight over you.

My loving God, the harp in my heart will praise you.
Your faithful heart toward us will be the theme of my song.
Melodies and music will rise to you, the Holy One of Israel.

PSALM 71:22

New opportunities are coming.

B eloved, you are in the dawning of a new season in your life. Have you felt the shifting of the winds? Instead of walking into the winds of adversity, the gentle breezes of my Spirit are now at your back. They will carry you along the path I have laid out for you straight into the open doors of destiny. It has not always been this distinct, and it won't always feel this easy. But daughter, in this season you will know the right direction to go, for I am leading you clearly.

What has been a mystery to you up until now will become obvious. Though you have agonized over decisions, trying to make the right choices, I will make the way in front of you unmistakable. Long-forgotten dreams will now enter your life in unexpected ways. This is my provision. You may not feel like you are enough, but you are equipped with everything you need to do this well. Open doors are before you. Even if you cannot see them yet, don't despair. It takes one moment of opportunity to fulfill a lifetime of questioning. Be persistent, and keep living. You cannot miss my goodness in this.

Knock, and the door will be opened for you. For every persistent one will get what he asks for. Every persistent seeker will discover what he longs for. And everyone who knocks persistently will one day find an open door.

MATTHEW 7:7–8

Fresh hope is dawning.

As the sun slowly creeps over the crust of the earth in the early morning dawn, so is my hope rising over you. The long night is over. Just watch and see, as your eyes adjust to the brightness of my faithful love, how all the details of what was hidden in the dark are now becoming visible. You are standing in the middle of a growing garden that you assumed was nothing but a wasteland.

See how the buds have formed on the flowers. They are getting ready to bloom. Look and see where you sowed in tears through the long dark night. There is extra growth there. I can't wait for you to see the incredibly lush beauty of the blossoms when they fully open. Nothing was wasted, my beloved, even when you could not make sense of the darkness. I was not simply consoling you in your pain and grief. I was tending to the garden of your heart, which you can now see is brimming to life again—and even more beautifully than before. Your heart will fill with joy as your hope tastes the sweet fruit of my faithful comfort. Take hold of my heart. Let me show you what has grown here so you can delight in the joy of a new day dawning.

Our faith guarantees us permanent access into this marvelous kindness that has given us a perfect relationship with God. What incredible joy bursts forth within us as we keep on celebrating our hope of experiencing God's glory!

ROMANS 5:2

Leave the past behind.

Beloved, open wide the doors of your heart and receive what I am speaking over you. Do not get tripped up by the mistakes of yesterday. Don't focus on the regrets of days gone by. Here, now, my mercy has washed you afresh. Today's portion is plentiful. Press on in love as I pursue your heart with my tender affection. This is a new opportunity for you to fix your eyes on what lies ahead of you—the treasure of my kingdom come and my will being done on the earth as it is in heaven.

Take hold of the invitation I have offered you, for there is abundant compassion to cover every failure and every misstep. I lead you on in loving-kindness. You won't be let down when you're living in the light of my glorious favor. Let my presence fill you with everything you need to run the race of this life with eyes fixed on me. I patiently lead you into the perfection of your faith as you follow me along the pathway of laid-down love. Keep going, daughter, for you have not reached the end of my kindness!

I do have one compelling focus: I forget all of the past as I fasten my heart to the future instead. I run straight for the divine invitation of reaching the heavenly goal and gaining the victory-prize through the anointing of Jesus.

PHILIPPIANS 3:13–14

Come alive in me.

I am the God who breathes life into dry bones and causes newness to spring from the ashes of defeat. I resurrect hopes buried in the soil of grief, and I cultivate new vines of sweet fruit by intertwining them with my faithful mercy. Let your heart take courage today in the life that is growing. You are awakening in the delight of my extravagant compassion again. Let the joy that has broken through the surface bubble up to overflowing!

Soak in the sunshine of my love. It fills you with all you need for an abundant life. It is time to draw back the curtains and let the fresh breeze of my Spirit clear out the staleness and dust of winter. Open up and let the light in. Allow me to remove all shadows, and you will feel sweet relief as my glorious light makes all things fresh and alive again. There is nothing stopping you now from reveling in my marvelous kindness. You have only to receive.

We know that the Son of God has made our understanding come
alive so that we can know by experience the One who is true.
And we are in him who is true, God's Son, Jesus Christ—
the true God and eternal life!

1 JOHN 5:20

I do not waver.

In these days of constant alteration and innovation, I want you to remember that I never, ever change. My character is the same firm foundation upon which I built the world in the beginning. Mercy as vast as the ocean covers my people. Fasten your heart to my love, and nothing will move your faith. Be anchored in the sea of my loving-kindness, and you will stay safe from overwhelming fear. Be rooted in my faithfulness, and your hope will remain secure.

Though seasons change and nations rise and fall, I am the I AM—who was, who is, and who is to come. I am Savior and King. I am the victorious One. I am the humble Lamb of God. There are many facets to my nature, but each remains constant as I am constant. You have tasted and seen my goodness in your life. Now take and eat the confidence of this reality: I am yours, and you are mine. I have chosen you as my own. My loyal love envelops you. There is no risk too great for you, for the current of my grace carries you. Whatever you do, let compassion cover it, for only love will stand the test of time. Be found in me, for I am your firm foundation.

Who guides the destiny of each generation
from the first until now?
I am the one! I am Yahweh, the first,
the unchanging one who will be there in the end!

ISAIAH 41:4

Leave your regret in the past.

Take my hand today as I lead you into the light of my mercy. It is the right time to lay down all of your old guilt. It is time to leave your shame behind and let me give you the garment of praise. As long as you carry around those reminders of your old ways, they will hold you back from growing into more of my goodness. Lighten your load as I offer you the yoke of my unfailing love.

My mercy covers every single one of your failures. Why would you hold yourself to account when I have forgiven you? Do you not trust that I am more powerful than the systems of this world? I have called you to a better life, to a higher way. It is the way of love that follows the path of radical trust in my character. Mercy is not for you to offer only to others. You must also be willing to let it cover every portion of your own story—both the seen and hidden parts. Step into the light of my life, child, and find your freedom in my unhindered affection.

I forget all of the past as I fasten my heart to the future instead. I run straight for the divine invitation of reaching the heavenly goal and gaining the victory-prize through the anointing of Jesus.

PHILIPPIANS 3:13–14

I come to your rescue.

Beloved, I will not let the trials that test you overtake you. They will not defeat your faith, nor will they demolish your hope. I am greater than the most powerful foe you could ever face. My love has conquered every fear with the strength of resurrection power. The same power that raised Christ from the grave to everlasting life is the very might of my Spirit who makes his home in you.

I will never leave you to fight your own battles, my child. Rest your trust in me, for my help is reliable. Even now, let your heart take courage in hope as you put all of your confidence in my faithful goodness. Do not be alarmed by the testing of your faith. All who follow me must live the human experience, so you will not escape pain in this life. But you will experience my constant comfort and powerful peace. My joy will be your strength, for there is not a moment where you are not the center of my delight. I am making a way for you in the wilderness seasons. I am your sustenance and strength and your ever-present help in times of trouble. Trust me; I won't let you go.

If the Lord Yahweh rescued Lot, he knows how to continually rescue the godly from their trials and to reserve the ungodly for punishment on the day of judgment.

2 PETER 2:9

Clothe yourself in prayer.

My dearly loved one, heed my Word today and turn yourself toward me with every question that arises in your heart. Let my truth fill your mind as you soak in my peaceful presence. There is nothing that you need to accomplish on your own. Instead, in all things, cover yourself in prayer. When you continually commune with me, your hope will remain strong.

It is never too late to implement the habit of constant communion. I offer you the fullness of my presence in every moment. I am always available to you. I note even the slightest whisper in my ledger. I keep track of every cry of your heart, and I see every desire and every calculated surrender of your will to mine. Abundant life is found in the laying down of your own limited ideas in favor of trust in my master plan. I do far more for you than you could ever do for yourself. As you practice a life of prayer, you train your heart to see my goodness at work in the details as well as the overarching story of your life. Whenever you think of it today, speak to me. I am always listening, and I have so much to share with you.

One day Jesus taught the apostles to keep praying
and never stop or lose hope.

LUKE 18:1

Keep going.

Beloved, have you grown weary of doing good? Are you tired of choosing what you believe to be the best without the return you long for? Come in close and let me refresh you in my presence. Let me fill you with the strength of my love that will more than sustain you. I have everything you need to press on in perseverance. Because I am leading you, child, you do not have to rely on your own limited resources to keep you going.

Let my mercy lift your burdens and fill your depleted reserves. Lean into my loyal love that continuously surrounds you. Follow my path of loving with abandon, for I will always replenish what you offer others. Do not give up or lose your hope, beloved. Rest here in my presence until you feel the vitality of my life flowing through your veins once more. Bathe in the warmth of my kindness that soaks into your soul and calms every anxious thought. I am your peace and your perfect portion. You can trust me because my path leads you to eternal glory.

Following your word has kept me from wrong.
Your ways have molded my footsteps, keeping me
from going down the forbidden paths of the destroyer.

PSALM 17:4

My heart is your home.

Come close and find your rest in the peace of my presence today. Though disappointments and setbacks mark your earthly relationships, I remain perfect in every way. My lavish love never misses the mark. Rather it seeps into every crack and crevice. Let me love you in a tangible way today, and let me show you how gracious and beautiful my kindness is.

There is no distance between us in this moment. I have not left you to tend to some other garden, for I am able to meet each one as she needs in every moment. All of my loyal lovers find their home in the fullness of my heart. Come find that you are wholly loved and have the longings of your heart met today. Let me speak my words of mercy and redemption over what you try to keep hidden in the recesses of your mind. I heal and restore everything—both the seen and unseen. Even now, I am speaking a better Word to you than anyone else ever will. You have been ushered into my kingdom, into my family, into my home. Don't hesitate at the perimeter of my presence but recklessly run into my open arms and be satisfied!

There is no power above us or beneath us—no power that could ever be found in the universe that can distance us from God's passionate love, which is lavished upon us through our Lord Jesus, the Anointed One!

ROMANS 8:39

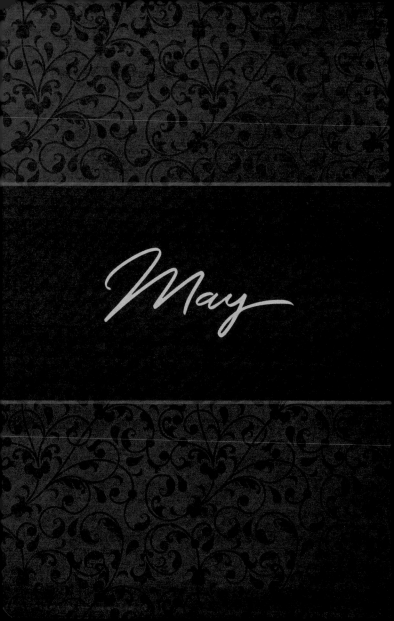

May

I won't let you go.

I n every season you face, in the triumphs and in the challenges, my great mercy surrounds you. No fear can overtake you, for my love already has. Let your own confidence grow as my faithfulness continually plays out in your life. I am your assurance, so place all of your hope in me. There is not a moment when my gracious grip over your life loosens. You are mine, beloved. I am caring for you in every season of the soul.

Trust me with your dreams. It is time to start working toward the goals that have been on the back burner. I will open doors as you run in the way of worthy ambitions. I will direct you as you look to me for guidance. I will teach you as you discern between what is worth your attention and what you should leave for another. Lean into my wisdom, and you will have understanding. Above all, no matter what, know that you will not wander outside of my unending kindness.

You have kept me from being conquered by my enemy;
you broke open the way to bring me to freedom,
into a beautiful, broad place.

PSALM 31:8

I see you in your pain.

My daughter, I am fully aware of the state of your heart today. I meet you in the midst of your messiest moments, and I never turn away. You already know that I don't require you to be strong on your own. When you are struggling, I don't want you to "get it together." If that's what you're hearing, then it's not my voice. I always offer comfort for your sorrow, healing for your wounds, and encouragement for discouragement.

I am not at a loss over what to do with you, child. I am not stumped about how to work my restoration in your life. I am more than able to take every disappointment and make it a springboard into greater hope. You have not been lost to your circumstances. Can't you see that I am with you here and now? There will be a great blessing where you have only been able to see the discomfort of an aching heart. Do not despair, for I am working in even the most devastating sorrows to bring comfort and redemption.

Even when their paths wind through the dark valley of tears,
they dig deep to find a pleasant pool where others find only pain.
He gives to them a brook of blessing
filled from the rain of an outpouring.

PSALM 84:6

I am for you.

Lean into my loyal love today, and let it surround you with the embrace of peace. I have not forgotten a single word that I have spoken over you. You can trust that I will be faithful all the days of your life and even beyond that. I am powerful enough to save my beloved ones from the snare of the enemy. No trap can keep my loyal lovers from experiencing the fullness of liberty in Christ.

I will rescue you every time trials surround you, and I will pick you up every time you fall. Nothing can keep you from the treasures that I have stored for you. You are my child, and I will always be your Advocate. You don't need to fight for yourself any longer if you will let me be your mighty defender. For I never fail. My justice is already on the way. I am working out redemption for ruin, restoration for loss, and hope for discouragement. I am for you, my child. Beauty for ashes is my offer in every disappointment. Will you participate in this holy exchange today?

He will appear as your righteousness,
as sure as the dawning of a new day.
He will manifest as your justice,
as sure and strong as the noonday sun.

PSALM 37:6

Peace is your portion.

Today I offer you the generous portion of my very present peace. In my Spirit, you have access to the atmosphere of my heart, which is the endless force of my gracious kindness. Let the peace of my presence calm the storms you have been battling in your mind. Let the calm of my steady heart settle the anxiety that threatens to keep you on endless alert. You can rest here in my arms knowing that I am taking care of everything that you cannot control.

Will you invite me in to the confusion you have been experiencing? I will bring order to the chaos and clarity in the light of my love. Trust me to do what you cannot, for I am the Alpha and Omega, and I never stop weaving my mercy into the fabric of this world. Rest in the confidence of my faithfulness, and you will feel joy return. My delight will flood your being with the hope of a better day. The worries of today will loosen their grip as you direct your gaze to my strong compassion that is already working for you. Press into peace, beloved, for it is yours to experience right here in this moment.

Whenever my busy thoughts were out of control,
the soothing comfort of your presence
calmed me down and overwhelmed me with delight.

PSALM 94:19

You are secure.

Let the confidence of my love be your firm foundation today. It is the rock that your life is built upon. You cannot escape my marvelous kindness, for I am working out my great grace in every triumph and every setback. Nothing can snatch you from my mercy. No trouble, trial, or storm is strong enough to carry you outside the parameters of my faithfulness.

I am a strong and steady place of refuge because I am not moved. There is no fear that I have not already overcome with my overwhelming grace. I see the end from the beginning and every moment in between. Find your trust in my unchanging goodness. Cast your cares on me today, for I care for you. Why let the worries of uncertainty take you down anxious pathways? Put your hope in me, for I am for you, and I always make a way for you even when you can't see one. I am clearing a path for you in the wasteland so that in the downpour of trials, you can always count on my light to guide you. The anchor of my strong love keeps you secure. I will never let you go.

The wicked are blown away by every stormy wind.
But when a catastrophe comes,
the lovers of God have a secure anchor.

PROVERBS 10:25

I am closer than a brother.

I n the ups and downs that this life may bring, you have something that no one can take away from you. I am your faithful friend, always there when you need me. I am your constant companion, never leaving your side. I am your ever-present Advocate, always promoting your best interests. Even when you feel alone and isolated, you are not. I do not abandon my loyal lovers. I am closer than your very breath.

Even if your own family were to disown you, I would never do such a thing. You can rely on my consistent kindness to counsel, comfort, and keep you. I am more reliable than the most devoted mother, and my love is more constant than the dawning of a new day. Feast on the rich fellowship of my Spirit and press into the abundance of my presence. I will never let you down. I am pure in motive and unrelenting in compassion toward you. You cannot exhaust my love, dear one. You are joined to my heart, both now and into eternity.

Some friendships don't last for long,
but there is one loving friend who is joined to your heart
closer than any other!

PROVERBS 18:24

I've got you.

Let your faith find its footing on the sure foundation of my strong love today. I am right here, child. I have not gone anywhere. But where there is doubt, let it float away on the winds of my mercy. I am more than able to deliver you from every struggle. Let my love carry you through this life, and there won't be a moment where you need give in to worry or apprehension. You will never lack anything you need, for I provide it all!

Let the turbulence of anxiety cease in the peace of my powerful presence. I am constant in compassion, always freely giving from the abundance of my loving-kindness. Keep following me on the path that you have been treading. It is not time to change course, but if you tune your heart into my own right now, I will release the revelation of my wisdom. I have a right-now word to encourage your soul. Lean in, child. Let your heart take hope in my unfailing love that leads you into the light of life.

Wrapping himself around me like a shield,
he is so generous with his gifts of grace and glory.
Those who walk along his paths with integrity
will never lack one thing they need, for he provides it all!

PSALM 84:11

You are held.

Lean back into the loving arms of your Bridegroom today. Find rest in my deep affection for you. Nothing could ever dissuade me from drawing you near. Like a devoted lover, I hold you close, delighting in your nearness. Find your rest here. I have no hidden motives. Only know that I am near and always here.

I will never force you to remain here, but the invitation I extend is yours for the taking. Will you let me love you to life again today? Will you allow my kindness to refresh your weary soul? Know that you can never push me away so far that I will not willingly welcome you back into my embrace. You can trust me. I am faithful. I won't ever leave. No matter how hard you fight against receiving my devoted affection, you cannot lessen its force. My passion does not dwindle over time. I will delight in your love with the same strength, no matter the state you're in. Will you let go of your hesitations today? I am love in its purest essence, and I made you in love's image.

His left hand cradles my head
while his right hand holds me close.
I am at rest in this love.

Song of Songs 2:6

You are my dearly loved daughter.

My beloved daughter, come close now and let me speak my words of affectionate kindness over you. I will remind you who you are. The depths of my delight are immeasurable, and my joy over you, my child, is indescribable. The light of your life is a beautiful reflection of the all-consuming fire of my love. My burning presence has marked you. You now have the living flame of my passion blazing inside of you.

There is not a moment where I hold back my kindness from you. As my child, you have free access to me. You always have a father's help when you need it. And I am no earthly father distracted by duties that I have to tend to. I am a perfect parent. I offer you everything you need right when it is required. I accomplish all of my purposes, and I have more than enough tireless attention to give to you whenever you call on me. Rise up in the confidence of my love today. Arise in the assurance of my unchanging character. I am your provision, and I have no lack of resources. You have unhindered access to abundant mercy. Live in the freedom of authority I have given you, child. And always trust me. I will not fail you.

Look with wonder at the depth of the Father's marvelous love that he has lavished on us! He has called us and made us his very own beloved children.

1 JOHN 3:1

The waves won't overtake you.

Just as I made a way through the Red Sea for the Israelites to cross to their freedom, so do I part the waters that keep you from liberation in your life. Nothing is impossible for me to do. Just as Jesus on the Sea of Galilee calmed the raging storm that threatened to sink the disciples' ship, you can also count on me to bring peace to the intense circumstances that threaten to take you out. The waves of adversity will not overtake you, and there is no chance that I would let you drown.

I uphold you with my mighty right hand, and I will not let you go. In every circumstance and in every season, I am your shield and your strength, and I will never let you be lost. Trust in me, child, and take confidence as you recognize my constant grip of grace on your life. My faithfulness to you is an unwavering covenant. Take courage, for I am with you—both now and always!

When you pass through the deep, stormy sea,
you can count on me to be there with you.
When you pass through raging rivers,
You will not drown.

ISAIAH 43:2

Trade your anxiety for peace.

In the landscape of my love is endless room to grow and explore. Come and discover the delight awaiting you. No hint of dread exists in my marvelous mercy, and my tender kindness is like a refreshing pool of the purest water you could imagine. Wade into its depths.

Today let your heart venture further into the serenity of my loving-kindness. Trade your anxiety for my persistent peace. Surrender your worries to me with confidence that I can handle every one of them. Don't believe the narrative that fear has been feeding you. Instead, feast on the wisdom of my perfect peace. My grace holds no trace of trickery, beloved. Find your courage in my unchanging character and in the goodness of my nature that will always faithfully reveal itself in your life. Open your eyes to see, and you will recognize that there is nothing that lies outside the realm of my resurrection power. Let your busy thoughts come to rest in the clarity of my life-giving light. There is nothing outside of my grasp. I see every detail of your life, and not a single one will go to waste. I use it all for your benefit. Trust me.

I leave the gift of peace with you—my peace.
Not the kind of fragile peace given by the world,
but my perfect peace.
Don't yield to fear or be troubled in your hearts—
instead, be courageous!

JOHN 14:27

Let me be your help.

D aughter, enter into the sanctuary of my presence today. Lean on my loyal love, and I will be your strong support. In your day of trouble, there is no better place to turn. My reserves are always full, and there is not a single situation that I am not prepared to help you through. I am your present and ever-faithful provision in every circumstance. You can rely on the power of my mercy to both cover and reinforce you.

You don't need to wage war against that which seeks to take you out. I will fight the battle for you. Hide in the refuge of my heart and join with my purposes as you praise your way to breakthrough. Choosing to honor me in your trials will make you more aware that the confidence of my character is the firm foundation you are already standing upon. Let my goodness strengthen your faith as you watch me work out my kindness in your life over and over again.

God, you're such a safe and powerful place to find refuge!
You're a proven help in time of trouble—
more than enough and always available whenever I need you.

PSALM 46:1

I am close.

No circumstance could make me decide to put distance between us. No complaint you could make would drive me away. In every heartbreak and in every disappointment, I am right by your side. My presence is your comfort. If you turn your attention to me for a moment, you will feel the warmth of my compassion enfolding you. I embrace you with my kindness and even more so in times of heartache.

Even in your sorrow, you can experience the deep relief of my present peace. Don't let your distress keep your heart at a distance. I am closer than your very breath, so open the gates of your heart to the healing oil of my love. Every word that departs from my lips drips with kindness. I am gentle, not demanding. In your suffering, I am the lifter of your head and the strength that holds you up. I will carry you when you cannot stay on your feet. I am your support. I don't require anything from you in this moment but a willing a heart. Will you open up to receive?

The Lord is close to all whose hearts are crushed by pain,
and he is always ready to restore the repentant one.

PSALM 34:18

Pursue my perspective.

Let me adjust your outlook as you turn your attention to me. My higher perspective takes in every detail that you miss as well as how they all connect to the bigger picture. Will you surrender the illusion of control today? Will you let go of your need to be right and instead pursue my truth with humility? I do not hide myself from you, beloved. I long for my wisdom to instruct your heart and your perspective. I want you to walk in the freedom that trusting me truly brings.

Today let the reality of my kindness at work in your life flood your mind. Look at the fruit of my faithfulness. I want to show you so much more. I will open up your understanding as you seek after my heart. I will saturate your soul with the vibrancy of my life in you. My Spirit breathes peace over your mind, so receive the clarity of my insight as you soak in my presence. There are no mysteries to me. Let me share with you my perfect perception. Let my living Word instruct your faith as you walk in my paths.

Help me turn my eyes away from illusions
so that I pursue only that which is true;
drench my soul with life as I walk in your paths.
PSALM 119:37

Live from my abundance.

Beloved daughter, I have given you access to everything you could ever need for abundant living. My lavish love is a continuously gushing river that covers everything in its path. You could not exaggerate my goodness. Come to me every new day and eat from my table of plenty. I have so much wisdom to share with you. I have peace beyond your comprehension ready to calm every fear. My mercy is your covering, both behind and before you. My compassion envelops your past, and your future is bright with the promise of my glory.

Don't hesitate to ask for more, child. It is my delight to fill you every time you ask. The satisfaction of my permeating presence will flood your life as you continue to turn toward me. Train your heart to rely on my faithfulness, and I will blow all of your expectations out of the water. You will be filled with joy overflowing as you bask in the delight of my affection. Don't hold back from me today, for I have told you that I certainly won't be stingy with my love!

A thief has only one thing in mind—he wants to steal, slaughter, and destroy. But I have come to give you everything in abundance, more than you expect—life in its fullness until you overflow!

JOHN 10:10

You are mine.

I have called you by name, child. You are mine. I know you better than you know yourself, including every motivation of your heart. There is no need to fear my love. It does not shame you, and it never degrades you. There is no competition in my love, either. Set your eyes on me, the author and finisher of your faith. The rushing river of my mercy engulfs you until there's nothing in your life that the power of my loving-kindness will leave untouched.

Let the roots of your hope go down deep in the soil of my faithful kindness. Your life is so very important to me that I desire for you to entwine within my very heart. Do not listen to the echoes of the deceiver who would have you believe that all is meaningless. I have brought you into my kingdom of light, so now is the time to let the glory of my goodness shine on your mind with revelation light. I will show you the incomprehensible joy of being loved and chosen by me. Open up and let the light in!

Do not fear,
for I, your Kinsman-Redeemer, will rescue you.
I have called you by name, and you are mine.

ISAIAH 43:1

You shine like a star.

Daughter, I have put my light inside of you. See how you shine! You are a beacon of my glory and an indicator of my presence among the living. My power is at work in your life, and it always has been. Look for the kernels of faith sown in the soil of your hardships. The resilience of your joy is beautifully flourishing. The fruit of my faithfulness in your story is evidence that I have marked you as my own.

Beloved one, you are a pure reflection of my radiance. Your love is beautiful. The way you pour yourself out for another's benefit clearly shows how much you look like me. Your perseverance in kindness and compassion is breathtaking to watch. None of it goes to waste. Watch as I water the seeds sown in laid-down love; they will produce a fruit sweeter than any you've tasted before. Your heart beautifully reflects my kingdom treasures, and any who are on the receiving end of your love gain blessings beyond measure. Every moment of self-sacrifice for the chance to support another in grace and strength is a testimony of my relentless kindness toward my children. How brightly you shine.

He lit every shining star and formed every glowing galaxy. …
He has numbered, counted, and given everyone a name.
They shine because of God's incredible power
and awesome might; not one fails to appear!

ISAIAH 40:26

I know the way through.

L et me pull you in closer to my side as we walk this winding path. I promise that I won't let you go. When the winds of uncertainty pick up, lean in close until you can hear the steady beat of my heart and feel my breath tickling the hairs on your head. I wrap my heavy cloak around you. Though the atmosphere has a biting chill, I tuck you into the warmth of my embrace.

Don't fear when you hear sirens in the distance. Don't break away and go off on your own, for I am leading you on the right path. When we get to the summit of this mountain, I will show you all that has been hidden up until now—the dangers you escaped as well as the treasures you picked up along the way. You will see how I protected you as you pressed into my side, hidden from the enemy's sight. You will see the glory that is right before us on the other side of this mountain, and you will receive so much rest, peace, and joy for your soul. So keep pressing into me as I lead you into glorious life with every step!

I will stay close to you,
instructing and guiding you along the pathway for your life. …
So don't make it difficult; don't be stubborn
when I take you where you've not been before. …
Just come with me!

PSALM 32:8–9

You are pursued by goodness.

I have written all the days of your life in my record. I see each one, and I have covered the entire timeline of your story with my wondrous mercy and great grace. Come, feast on my goodness again. Your portion of provision is plentiful. I am pursuing you with goodness all the days of your life. I have granted you full access to my presence in every moment. Don't hesitate, daughter. You have a free audience with the King of kings—your Father God—anytime you turn your attention toward me.

Come freely now. Enter in with thanksgiving. Here I have all that you've been looking for. See how I have taken care of the lilies of the fields and the birds of the air. I take even more thoughtful care of you. For you are my precious daughter, a jewel in my crown. So throw off the worries and abandon the overbearing burdens of control. I have everything you need. I am taking care of you. Find your freedom in the glorious light of my affection today and every day. You cannot escape my goodness, for you are my own!

Take the carefree birds as your example. ...
God takes care of every one of them,
feeding each of them from his love and goodness.
Isn't your life more precious to God than a bird?
Be carefree in the care of God!

LUKE 12:24

I am immoveable.

B uild all your hope upon the rock-steady foundation of my unchanging character. Place all your bets on my faithfulness. Nothing can thwart my purposes, and nothing can put out the passionate affection of my heart. My loving nature holds the universe together. What I do, no one can undo.

I am the all-consuming fire, and I am also refreshing waters of peace. I am Defender, provider, and Advocate. I am also justice-keeper, Holy One, and righteous judge. I am faithful Father, merciful mother and long-standing lover. In me, all of creation finds its source and satisfaction. Every created being is a reflection of my kindness. I always know the best way out of a challenging situation. Do you doubt my perfect plans? Child, I am for you, and you are mine. Whatever relationships you have in your life, don't you know that you find its perfect match in me? My unfailing love is your lifeblood. Look to me today, and I will show you things that you have not seen before. I will give you revelation to recognize what you have not understood up until now. Stand now under the waterfall of my Spirit-life as I pour out my living understanding over you.

You are "I AM."
You never change, years without end!
HEBREWS 1:12

I am clearing a pathway.

I am the God of all wisdom. I make ways in the wilderness and paths in the wastelands. Can you see that I am going before you into the great unknown? Daughter, take courage, for nothing is a mystery to me. You can rely on my perfect leadership to guide you every step of the way. The light of my living Word is a lamp to your feet so that even in the black of night, you can trust that I see things clearly. I will always show you the way to go.

Trust my faithfulness as you journey in this life. If you stumble, I catch you with my strong hand. I won't let you slip away. If you forget who I am, look to the testimonies of my people throughout the ages. Remember your own history—the paths we've walked together. Have I failed you yet? Have I left you to fend for yourself? I tell you, no. My presence will never leave you, daughter, for you are mine. What seems impossible to you is an opportunity for you to walk forward in faith. Just watch and see how I lead you through this covered in my mercy-love!

Your steps formed a highway through the seas
with footprints on a pathway no one even knew was there.

PSALM 77:19

Generosity leads to favor.

I created you in the image of lavish love. There is more than enough for all to draw from my wells of living water. As the power of my merciful kindness continuously fills you up, let it overflow into the lives of those around you. And don't stop with the inadvertent spilling over of compassion. You have been filled up to pour out. Don't hold back. There is always more to satisfy. When you are running low, be sure to turn to me. I will always replenish your stores of compassion. Be satisfied in the steady stream that my Spirit pours over you.

And when you are satisfied, pour out the blessing on others. Don't hold back from releasing my life through yours with the likeness of my glorious grace. Give without expecting anything in return. Love without hidden motive. Let your life reflect the purity of my purposes, with sacrifice laced with compassion as your lifestyle. Your reward will be great, for it will come straight from my kingdom. As you live generously, so delight in the abundance of Spirit-fruit evident in your life.

Those who live to bless others
will have blessings heaped upon them,
and the one who pours out his life to pour out blessings
will be saturated with favor.

PROVERBS 11:25

You are written on my heart.

B eloved, you could not exaggerate the scope of my love for you. It is immeasurable. The tablet of my heart holds the names of all my loyal lovers. My affection is inclusive, and it does not discriminate based on nationality or race. It does not love the well-behaved more than the struggling souls. Can't you see that my lavish love is bigger and better than your finite fondness? I do not say this to shame you but to open your understanding to how great my love is.

A mother does not forget the child that she bore, and even if she somehow did, I could never forget you. I have carved you into my own flesh. You are ever before me, never hidden from my sight. Are you beginning to comprehend how this works? Let your heart take courage in the confidence of my grave-robbing love. You are my daughter, my family, my kin. I see you. I'm with you. I am for you. Let the boldness of your identity grow brighter as you let my presence surround and strengthen you in ever-increasing measure.

I could never, no never, forget you. Can't you see?
I have carved your name on the palms of my hands!

Isaiah 49:15–16

Fellowship with my Spirit.

Come close and hear what I have to say over you today, child. Christ has given you unhindered access to me. You have fellowship with me, here and now, through the gift of my Holy Spirit. Let the life of my Spirit fill you as you practice the awareness of my presence with you. And it is a practice. Think about what it is to train a thought, to take it captive and to examine it. In the same way, when you bring your awareness to the present moment, you teach yourself to tune into the subtleties of the here and now.

Right now, take a moment with me. Close your eyes, release the tension from your shoulders, and turn your attention to your breath. As you breathe in, imagine that you are breathing in my perfect peace. As you breathe out, picture that you are releasing all anxiety and doubt. Keep doing this. And then turn your attention to the sensation of the air on your skin. Let your mind picture perfect love wrapping around you like a warm blanket. This is what I offer you in Spirit and in truth. To imagine it is to realize that it is already so. Stay as long as you can, resting and fully aware of the presence of endless mercy.

May the grace and joyous favor of the Lord Jesus Christ,
the unambiguous love of God, and the precious communion
that we share in the Holy Spirit be yours continually.

2 CORINTHIANS 13:14

I use humble things.

C hild, come close and let me remind you of my gracious power at work in your life. There is no greater force moving through this world than the power of my redemption breathing life into areas of destruction and decimation. And you, my daughter, are a partner in my wonder-working plan. Before you protest, beloved, let me remind you of my track record. Your qualifications exist in your identity as my own. You have already experienced the power of my love in your life, so join your experience to build your faith.

Do you not already know that I use the humble to confound those who are wise in their own eyes? Pride may push a person along to a certain point, but it is a dead end. Keep your heart humble, and you will never have to worry about your position in me. I give you all the strength you could ever require, and you can be certain that the wisdom I offer is better than the knowledge of all the world's scholars. You are lacking no good thing. Trust me and take my hand.

God chose those whom the world considers foolish to shame those who think they are wise, and God chose the puny and powerless to shame the high and mighty.

1 Corinthians 1:27

I am dancing with delight.

As light dances on everything that comes into its path, so do I reach you with the rays of my loving-kindness. When light mingles with mist, it forms the symbol of my faithful promise that I gave after the great flood. Rainbows are a reminder of my covenant that cannot be broken. They are a sign of peace and of hope. What child does not fill with wonder when they spot one?

In the same way, know that I am dancing over you with joy. Whenever you feel deep delight, it is but a small reflection of my glorious pleasure. I enjoy you with the love of an enchanted parent watching his child move in the world. Let go in my love and enjoy the goodness that is available to you right now. My Spirit revives your inner world with light and life. Can you feel the delight springing up from the fellowship of my living Word inside of you? Share in my joy by joining in the dance of life and liberty today!

The princes of God's feasts will sing and dance, singing,
"Every fountain of delight springs up from your life within me!"

PSALM 87:7

Let me fight your battles.

L isten to me, daughter. Do you not know? Have you not heard? I am the God who holds the world in his hands, the source of life itself. I am the same One who sets captives free, raises the dead to life, and causes nations to rise and fall. And still I am your God and Father. Loosen your feeble grip of control and let me fight for you as you rest in my mercy.

Trust me as I go to battle for you. I will not let slander overtake you, and I won't let the hatred of others knock you down. Remember that you cannot escape my grace, beloved, because you're living in it. Hide yourself in my Word and find comfort in my Spirit's nearness. I am quenching the fiery arrows of the enemy with my shield. Don't worry. My mercy is large enough to both defend and liberate you. Rest in me and trust that I will keep you safe. Do not abandon integrity in the midst of this. Hold your position: steady in love. You will make it through.

Here he stands! The Commander! The mighty Lord of Angel Armies is on our side! The God of Jacob fights for us!

PSALM 46:11

Rest in my confidence.

Bring your heart to me and be encouraged. There is no better moment to take hold of the hope to which I have called you. Rest assured that I am faithfully working out my promises in the earth. My beloved ones are living in the light of my goodness. Bind your faith to my loyalty, and you will never be disappointed. Rest in the confidence of my consistent character, and the winds of adversity will not shake you. You can rely on my fixed focus. Don't worry; I cannot be distracted from my purposes or talked out of my merciful plans.

Take stock of my dependability, if you must. But don't forget to align it with my nature. There are details that the naked eye will miss. But my perfect perspective holds everything in account. Trust my heart and you will be confident in my ways. I have not forgotten a single request from you. I have not forsaken a single promise. Rest in my grace today and watch me work it all out!

Those of us who believe, faith activates the promise
and we experience the realm of confident rest!

HEBREWS 4:3

Join in my heavenly celebration.

There is no need to wait to join in the celebration of heaven. Through fellowship with my Spirit, you have been ushered into a new kingdom that does not fail. There is joy to be had in my presence, so jump on in. Join the song that I sing over you, bringing you into freedom. It is the song of the redeemed.

Let your heart fill with the delight of my own that beats with the rhythm of my loyal lovers coming home. My heart has no shortage of pleasure, and so it is my desire that my people have no shortage of pleasure. Let your soul find its pure bliss in communion with me, echoing the multitudes that have gone before. You belong to an everlasting kingdom with the morning star as its radiance. My light will forever shine on my beloved ones. So lay down your burdens and lift up your praise today.

By contrast, we have already come near to God in a totally different realm, the Zion-realm, for we have entered the city of the Living God, which is the New Jerusalem in heaven! We have joined the festal gathering of myriads of angels in their joyous celebration!

HEBREWS 12:22

Place your hope in me.

Beloved, take heart today. There is no obstacle that I haven't already overcome. There is no challenge you face that I haven't already dealt with. Place all your trust in me as you wait for me to come through for you. In the waiting time, press into the perfect peace of my presence. I am closer than you know. Even now, I surround you with songs of deliverance. I will always lead you to breakthrough!

When you don't know what else to do, put your hope in me. I am faithful and true, I am constant in love, and I am strong in mercy. No one can repeal my judgments, and my justice stands firm. Wait on me. Put your hope in me and trust that I am with you and I will never abandon you, my child. I wrap you up in my mighty mercy. I tuck you into my tender kindness. You are safe and secure here. Let me awaken your heart to the sweetness of my love here in the shaky places. Don't worry, for only those things that can be shaken will be. But I am not one of those things. I will not be moved, and you will not be lost.

I will wait for the Lord Yahweh,
who hides his face from the family of Jacob.
And I will place all my hope in him!

ISAIAH 8:17

I have gone before you.

My child, let your heart rest in trust today. Every place that your feet will tread, I have already gone. It is true that I never leave you, and still I am able to be behind and before. There are no mysteries to me. I see it all clearly—the end from the beginning and every space in between. Stand on the confidence of my character. It is tried and true. I have never wavered in love, not even for a moment. You are my beloved, and I am leading you in loving-kindness.

Fix your eyes on me. Instead of allowing the questions of what may or may not happen consume you, why not trust the One who already knows? I will not let you fall because I already see clearly where I am leading you. Trust my goodness to cover you. There is no path you could tread that does not know my footprint. Follow me. No matter what challenges arise, I will be with you with all the wisdom and comfort you need until your feet cross into the forever glory of my kingdom.

Our anchor of hope is fastened to the mercy seat which sits
in the heavenly realm beyond the sacred threshold,
and where Jesus, our forerunner, has gone in before us.

HEBREWS 6:19–20

June

Rest today.

I am the source of all life—the Beginning and the End. I hold everything together with the power of my love. Come into my presence today with open arms, for I will take your heavy burdens and lead you into my rest. There is peace to restore your weary soul. Take a break from the distractions of this life that lead to unnecessary worrying. Whatever is going on in your world, take rest in me today. Though you cannot control a single outcome, I know every winning strategy.

Find refreshment in the pool of my living love today. Here, there is satisfaction for your needs and relief for your restlessness. There is no pressure in my presence—nothing to inhibit the joy of being fully known and accepted. I love you more than you can comprehend. I will never stop lavishing my mercy-kindness over your life. Give in to the current of my compassion that covers your mistakes and your failures. You are drenched in my Spirit, so be rejuvenated by my life inside of you. Let it spring up anew!

As we enter into God's faith-rest life we cease from our own works, just as God celebrates his finished works and rests in them.

HEBREWS 4:10

Your urgent help is here.

Let your heart take courage in the words of life I am offering you in this moment. Come boldly to my throne whenever you need help. As surely as the sun rises in the east, so will I come through for you. I will never turn you away, for you are mine. My power is made perfect in your weakness. I will never leave you to let the current of fear and hopelessness overtake you. I am your great Defender and your forever Advocate.

You have tasted and seen my goodness before, but I tell you the truth—you will feast on the richness of my mercy until you are satisfied. I offer you grace to empower you in strength so that you will recognize my Spirit-power at work in you. What I offer is unmatched by any smooth-talkers. You already know that self-ambition does not tarnish my love. I freely pour it out without hidden motive. Stand under the falls of my kindness and be refreshed once again as I fight your battles. Your help is at hand.

Now we come freely and boldly to where love is enthroned,
to receive mercy's kiss and discover the grace we urgently need
to strengthen us in our time of weakness.

HEBREWS 4:16

My goodness surrounds you.

Beloved, turn your ear to my voice today. My love calls to you and beckons you to come. Can you hear me calling you higher? I will give you my perspective in place of your limited view. Come, let me show you how I have surrounded you with my goodness, how I have encircled your life in my mercy. You are living inside of my great grace.

I am weaving the different threads of your life together with the cord of my kindness. You cannot escape the treasure of my Spirit-life working all things together for your good and benefit, beloved. There is nothing wasted in my hands. My power is made perfect in your weakness. Even what you deem to be your biggest failures are but fodder for my redemptive work. Just you wait and see what I will do with the ashes of those failures. I am cultivating beauty from them even now. Can you sense the new life growing here? Let your heart take hope today and rise up to meet my grace. Let the dejection of disappointment lift as you see from my perfect perspective. I am not idle, not even for a moment.

We are convinced that every detail of our lives is continually woven together to fit into God's perfect plan of bringing good into our lives, for we are his lovers who have been called to fulfill his designed purpose.

ROMANS 8:28

Worry is a waste of energy.

Let your heart take hope today in the stream of my living love. Come lay down your cares at my feet. Let me lift the burdens that have been weighing you down. Sit and feast at my table of plenty. Eat of my tender kindness that breaks down the strongest defenses. Drink of my mercy that satisfies every lack and clears out all shame. Partake of my power that infuses you with energy and passion to accomplish all that you hope and dream.

There is no need to keep a running account of possibilities that may or may not happen in your life or in the lives of those you love. I am already aware of every eventuality, and I will supply you with all you need for every moment. Why rely on your limited resources when you have access to a boundless reserve? Be partnered with me, and you will never need to be dependent on your ability alone. I am able to do far more than you could ever imagine. Fear will not overtake you, for my love already has. Trust me!

> Don't worry or surrender to your fear.
> For you've believed in God,
> now trust and believe in me also.
>
> JOHN 14:1

Speak words of life.

A s my child, you are a reflection of me in your world. Let your heart be encouraged today to align with my heavenly ways and my kingdom purposes. Remember who you are and who you were always meant to be. As a child of the light, shine bright. Let the words of your mouth reflect the compassion of my heart. Let your speech be full of life-giving encouragement and truth. Do not propagate fear or join with those who curse others.

You are a daughter of the living God who is full of mercy toward all. Honor others and imitate me by extending the same loving-kindness. Be a seeker of the good and a promoter of peace in all you do. Bless others and do not tear them down. Even in the face of adversity, let your words reflect the kindness that consumes you because the all-consuming fire of my love has marked you. If you live this way, you will live in the fullness of my goodness. No accusation made against you will stand. Let the light of your faith shine purely through your conscious choices.

Do you want to live a long, good life,
enjoying the beauty that fills each day?
Then never speak a lie or allow wicked words
to come from your mouth.

PSALM 34:12–13

Celebrate the growth.

My daughter, today is the day of jubilation. It is a day for celebrating. You have not been lost to the darkness that closed around you. The sea of sadness that flowed into your life with pain, grief, loss, and death did not sweep you away. Look at where you are, standing in your courage. Look how far we've come. You are not a slave to fear, and you are no longer afraid of the shadows. You are living in the confidence of my goodness over you. My intentions for you have always been full of affectionate joy. You cannot imagine what I have in store for you. But I promise you, it is immeasurably good.

Fall back into my arms of compassion again and let me love you to life. Drink in my delight. My dear one, I will never turn you down when you ask for more of me. You don't have to question my affection, for it is more abundant than you could ever imagine. I love you more than the world can contain. There is no way that you could ever reach the end of my love, for it has no measure.

> Then he broke through and transformed all my wailing
> into a whirling dance of ecstatic praise!
> He has torn the veil and lifted from me
> the sad heaviness of mourning.
> He wrapped me in the glory garments of gladness.
>
> PSALM 30:11

You are my child.

You have been born of an eternal kingdom-realm that knows no limitations. You are my dearly-loved child, the apple of my eye. Bask in the warmth of my delight that radiates even brighter than the sun. When you aligned your life with Jesus, you broke every agreement that kept you bound by fear and shame. I declared you clean in the cleansing blood of the Lamb. My Word remains the last, and there is none more powerful. No one can make a claim on you, for you are mine!

I always look out for my own. Don't hold back from running into my presence every chance you get. Just a turn of your attention and you will realize that I am always ready to commune with you through my Spirit. Bring me every need you have, for I am your provider. You have access to the abundance of my kingdom, so don't hesitate. Live in the freedom of what it means to be a child of the living God and fellowship with your maker!

God himself will fill you with more. Blessings upon blessings will be heaped upon you and upon your children from the maker of heaven and earth, the very God who made you!

PSALM 115:14–15

My love liberates.

There is no area of your life left untouched by my lavish love. It heals all your diseases, awakens the sleepiest hopes, and sets your heart ablaze with passion. It fills in the cracks of disappointment, lifts the hanging head of heartbreak, and floods the dry and weary places with living waters of refreshing. Yield to the tide of this love today and find yourself freed from the chains of shame that kept dragging you down. Fear and shame are liars that would keep you small, but my mercy has already opened the doors of every prison. Rise up in your freedom!

Since my love is more than enough for you, there is no reason to live in scarcity. Draw from my deep wells of delight. Drink your fill. Water your gardens and then water your neighbor's while you're at it. You have more than you could ever think to ask me for available to you right here and right now. Let the abundance of my Spirit-life flood your mind and heart with the living water of my presence. Come alive in my love!

The Spirit of the Lord is upon me, and he has anointed me to be hope for the poor, freedom for the brokenhearted, and new eyes for the blind, and to preach to prisoners, "You are set free!" I have come to share the message of Jubilee, for the time of God's great acceptance has begun.

LUKE 4:18–19

I lead you to rest.

Take my hand and let me guide you now into my perfect peace. My rest is always available to you through surrender and trust in my constant character. No matter the storms that rage, I am the calm in the chaos. I never change, and I never will. I will keep you in peace as you keep your gaze fixed on me.

Look to me, daughter, and you will not be dissatisfied. My eyes are full of fiery love for you at all times. I offer you the fullness of my affection no matter what is happening in or around you. Trust in my unfailing love and lean back into the harmony of my heart. Lay your worries aside as you place all your hopes in me. I will not betray your trust. I am confident in my intent and approach. My ways will not waver in the face of opposition. I am faithfully working all things out for the benefit of my beloved ones. I am the master restorer, always redeeming what the enemy means for harm and producing sweet fruit out of the ashes of disappointment. Rest in hope now; I have got this.

God is your confidence in times of crisis,
keeping your heart at rest in every situation.

PROVERBS 3:26

I will reveal the way.

Daughter, do you lack insight today? Come to me and I will give you the wisdom and guidance you are searching for. Put the hand of your trust in my capable grasp. Even darkness is as light to me. Therefore nothing can take me by surprise. Lean into my love and let your heart rest in the confidence of my faithful character. I am full of understanding, and you will find the completion of your own searching in who I am. I am fullness, and I am the fulfillment of every longing.

Trust me to guide you into my goodness. Even the barren places will become lush with the fruit of my presence. I will lead you along the pathway of my peace. You are hemmed into the garment of my mercy. But don't be discouraged. It is full of space for you to run in the freedom of my delight. You cannot escape my glory, for you are living in its light. When you cannot see the way, hold tight to me and follow my lead. It's all clear to me.

The word from heaven will come to us with dazzling light to shine upon those who live in darkness, near death's dark shadow. And he will illuminate the path that leads to the way of peace.

LUKE 1:79

I am the God of miracles.

The same God who hung the stars in the sky and breathed life into dry bones is the One who calls you his own. I am the God of Moses, who led the Israelites on a dry path through the Red Sea. I am the God of David, who killed a giant with a pebble and a slingshot. I am the God of Esther, who delivered a nation through humility coupled with courage.

I am also your God, writing your story with my love and miracle-working power. There are signs and wonders that you have yet to see with your own eyes. My power at work in your life will broaden your experience. When you see a dead end, it is a perfect opportunity to press into my heart with trust. I will instruct you in faith, and I will do what you can only imagine if you let your passion run into the boldness of my unfailing love. As you tell others about my goodness, I will back you up with evidence of the things only I can do. Let your expectations rise as I overshoot every one of them!

Then God added his witness to theirs. He validated their ministry with signs, astonishing wonders, all kinds of powerful miracles, and by the gifts *of* the Holy Spirit, which he distributed as he desired.

HEBREWS 2:4

I am with you in the wilderness.

When you enter a season of wilderness where all of your hopes are tested, I will be with you. There is not a single situation where I would abandon one of my loyal lovers. I will do what you could never dream of doing on your own. I will display miracles, dreams, and powerful signs and wonders on your behalf. It will be a place of discovery, even in the midst of devastation. This is the place where you learn to decipher my voice from all others. I will reveal myself to you as I did to Moses in the burning bush.

No matter what forces come against you, I will be your defense. I will provide for every single need you have. Rest in my presence until you can feel the might of my mercy strengthen your feeble faith. I will not leave you. When you look back on the wilderness from the other side, you will see a garden of sweet fruit where once you could only perceive barrenness. Take courage, for the God of Abraham, Isaac, and Jacob is your God.

In mercy you have seen my troubles and you have cared for me;
even during this crisis in my soul I will be radiant with joy,
filled with praise for your love and mercy.

PSALM 31:7

You are hidden in Christ.

My daughter, your life is hidden away in me. Though you cannot escape your own humanity as long as you tread the earth this side of eternity, you can know the all-surpassing peace of my presence that cares for you in every moment. The cleansing blood of Christ is your covering. No one can take you out from under mercy's tide. Find your rest here in the hidden place where my Spirit fellowships with yours.

Let the tranquility of my unwavering love fill your heart today. When you feel exposed and vulnerable, retreat in your heart to the quiet place where your deep need calls out to the even deeper kindness of my affection. I minister peace as you find your security in my unfailing compassion. I wrap around you with the comfort of my ever-present love. This is the place where you and I are one, where the winds of this world will never move my Spirit, which lives in you. You can rely on my steady hand of grace to keep you covered all the days of your life.

Your crucifixion with Christ has severed the tie to this life,
and now your true life is hidden away in God in Christ.

COLOSSIANS 3:3

I have not forgotten you.

Daughter, draw near to my heart of love today. I am here now, surrounding you with my presence. I have not left you for a moment. No, not for a single second. Be still and know now that I am your God. I delight in your attention more than a thousand sacrifices offered in my name. I am with you every step of this journey. In the tender moments of sorrow and vulnerability, I am not forcing faith upon you. I am not a demanding Father.

I have written you on the palm of my hand, and nothing could distract me from my plans and purposes for you. Who can bring my righteousness into question? Do you think a case that maligns my character stands a chance of victory? I tell you plainly, there is no one who knows the true depths of my mercy or the lengths of my loving-kindness. I am infinitely better than you assume, daughter. Will you let me lead you on in love as I reveal the hidden treasures that have yet to be mined on your path to glory? Trust me. I am with you, and I am for you.

Your righteousness is unmovable, just like the mighty mountains.
Your judgments are as full of wisdom as the oceans are full of
water. Your tender care and kindness leave no one forgotten,
not a man nor even a mouse.

PSALM 36:6

Surrender your convenience.

Beloved, hear the tenderness in my voice as I instruct you in my worthy ways today. Why are you holding so tightly to your plans for your life? Do you not know that I know you better than you know yourself? You can trust me to guide you into goodness, which will taste sweeter than anything you've experienced yet. Daughter, being comfortable is not a value of my kingdom. Convenience is not better than compassion. Surrender your fears about losing your comfort, and I will show you a bigger and brighter future!

Do you forget that all-surrendering love marks my path? Whenever you submit your own will to mine, I will lead you into places that require courage. I guide you into the unknown where all is familiar to me though you may struggle to believe that's enough. My faithfulness will put your fears to rest as it continues to work out in your life. Though change comes, you can always trust me to be with you through it all. Don't resist the inevitable shifts. Rather turn your gaze toward me again and again. There is no lack of assurance in my love.

All who are obsessed with being secure in life will lose it
all—including their lives. But those who let go of their lives
and surrender them to me will discover true life.

LUKE 17:33

I am the Morning Star.

The light of my love has risen on you, and you are living in its radiance. Walk in the way of my perfect peace and follow the light of my very-present kindness. You have heard my voice, so you know that it is like rushing waters, refreshing you with pure life every time I speak. You know that condemnation and shame are not markers of my correction. Every word that says you are in deep darkness beyond my reach is a lie and a trick. Align yourself today in my love's light. Do you not remember the joy of the freedom you felt at first? Let it rise up within you once more, for it is your right as my child to always live in the pure delight of my affection.

Let holy hope flood your heart and mind as you lift up consecrated hands toward me once more. This is where you find the life you've always wanted—in the liberty of my love. Surrender to my kindness, and you will always have more than you could ever imagine. I am your source and your lifeblood. Your life grows sweet fruit in the light of my goodness.

I, Jesus, sent my angel to you to give you this testimony
to share with the congregations. I am the bright Morning Star,
both David's spiritual root and his descendant.

REVELATION 22:16

Don't detest the testing.

Beloved, come close now as I speak to you. When you are in the times of testing that come with your humanity, trust me. Seek me out, and you will discover that I am there in the middle of every mess you find yourself in. You cannot escape trials in this life, but you can find peace in every one of them by clinging to me. My strong love is a beacon of hope in the midst of raging storms. I will never let you go, and I won't leave you for even a moment.

I never abandon my own. My Word shows that I will always be faithful. No storm lasts forever, and I will be with you through the whole thing. Look to me, beloved. Hide in the shadow of my garment. I will pull you close into my side, covering you in my comfort. If you have questions, ask them. Don't build walls of disappointment around your heart when you have unhindered access to mine. I promise that I will lead you through with my faithful love.

We all experience times of testing,
which is normal for every human being.
But God will be faithful to you. ...
And each test is an opportunity to trust him more.

1 Corinthians 10:13

I am preparing all things.

I have led you along the pathway of my peace as you have followed me. I have already walked every step. I have gone before you, preparing the way. Even in stormy weather, you could depend on my kindness to cover you and hide you deep in my heart. In my mercy, I have also followed behind and tied up the loose ends of your past into my loving-kindness. There is nothing in your past or future that is untouched by my power.

Trust me as I continue to lead you in love. There is nothing that can escape my redemption work or my restorative power. After all, I am the God who resurrects. My hand of love is upon you all the days of your life. You are immersed in my mercy. Take hope, daughter, for I am leading you into my goodness. You are ready for everything that comes your way, for you have me as your constant companion and guide, and I am always prepared!

You've gone into my future to prepare the way, and in kindness you follow behind me to spare me from the harm of my past. With your hand of love upon my life, you impart a blessing to me.

PSALM 139:5

I turn deserts into gardens.

When you walk through barren valleys, you will find that I am near, guiding you along the pathway of my peace. As you tread the desolate land, my goodness will meet you even there. Your desert will become a place of lush growth. For I am the God who turns deserts into gardens. I will turn your wastelands into forests. There is no landscape that your submission and my lavish love will not touch and flourish.

Trust me in the trying times. I am nearer than you know. Press into my presence, and I will be there, closer than the air, closer than the skin on your bones. I will sustain you, guide you, and I will grow you in confidence in my unfailing love. My power will work the impossible in your life. Do not be afraid of the dry and dusty deserts, for it is in these places you will see and experience the most amazing transformations. A desert is a place of testing and of surrender. It is a place of leaning on me, your beloved. Just you wait and see, love. You will be astonished as you feast on the fruit of fallen dreams. It will be sweeter than you could ever hope!

The desert will blossom like a rose and rejoice!
Every dry and barren place will burst forth with abundant blossoms.

ISAIAH 35:1–2

Listen to my living words.

L et the light of my wisdom fill your thoughts as you open up your heart before me today. Will you trust that my insights are sufficient to train you in a life of wisdom? My understanding is unmatched. Nothing goes overlooked in my sight. I see what others miss. No one on earth has full revelation of the details of all creation. I can read hearts like you read books. Will you let me into your heart? I offer you perfect peace in every circumstance, and I will never change my mind.

Lean on my unfailing love as I lead you through the darkness of moonless nights. Hold on to me as I guide you. Listen for my voice, and you will always know which way to turn. I will not let you be lost. I know what I'm doing, and I know how to get you through every difficulty. I have not made my pathway an obstacle course, though you will have to trust me and lean on me when the path gets rough. Depend on my loyal love, no matter what, and you will see goodness in every single season.

I delight to fulfill your will, my God, for your living words
are written upon the pages of my heart.

PSALM 40:8

Your foundation will not be shaken.

Your life is built upon the solid rock of my salvation. My love has set you free, and you have chosen to construct your hopes on the firm foundation of my mercy. You are standing on my unchanging character, on my nature that clearly declares the faithfulness of my ways. There is no need to fear, in any season or storm, when you plant your feet in my loyal love. And planted they are!

Everything that can be shaken will be. When the trembling cracks the façade of safety and comfort in your earthly dwelling, look to me, to the One who cannot be shaken. Throw all your cares on me. I will never turn away, not even for a moment. Your life is hidden in Christ, and what is eternal can never be taken away. Take hope, for I have overcome the world. You are overcoming, even in the shaking, when you don't give up. Look to me when you are afraid and be assured. I say it again, look to me.

This phrase "once and for all" clearly indicates the final removal of things that are shaking, that is, the old order, so only what is unshakeable will remain.

HEBREWS 12:27

You are clean.

Daughter, you have been washed in the blood of the Lamb, and you are clean. Nothing in your life remains untouched by my marvelous mercy. The cleansing flow of my lavish love covers you, and you cannot escape its power. I make all things new, including you. Let the wonder of my Spirit-life within you flood your heart with joy as I reveal my overwhelming delight over you.

Who can bring any grounded accusations against your destiny when your life is hidden in Christ? You are mine, and no one can steal your identity as my child. You are a coheir with Christ, a beneficiary of my kingdom. You will grow in the wisdom of your standing as you continue to fellowship with me. Seek my truth, and you will find it. Throw off everything that hinders the liberty of love in your life and run with endurance the race set out before you, hand in hand with me. Drink of my deep delight, for it is living water that satisfies every thirst.

When I look at you, I see how you have taken my fruit and tasted my word. Your life has become clean and pure, like a lamb washed and newly shorn. You now show grace and balance with truth on display.

SONG OF SONGS 4:2

Soak in my light.

T he warmth of love's light is shining upon you. Awaken and arise and see that I have fixed my affectionate gaze upon you. Everything else pales in comparison to the strength of my mercy. Let the strong rays of my kindness purify your heart as you soak in my presence. You will find true life in me. Your freedom is here in the intimate exchange of fellowship through Christ. Who else can read your heart the way I do? Who can infuse you with the strength of pure love through my Spirit?

You come alive here in my light, so make this your home. Camp here in my presence, and you will eat of my wisdom and drink of my delight. The world can offer you nothing better. Trust me. I am the One who created it all, so what you're looking for you will find only in me. You don't have to go searching the world for the beauty that is yours here, now, in the light of my presence. With the living God as your guide, you will never want for anything. I will satisfy you with the rich fruit of my Spirit-life.

Jesus said, "I am light to the world and those who embrace me will experience life-giving light, and they will never walk in darkness."

JOHN 8:12

My beauty rests on you.

Beloved one, the splendor of my marvelous mercy rests on you today. You are full of my glory. My Spirit, alive in you, bursts forth and lights your whole life like the sun breaking through the clouds. You are mine, and you shine like a star in the heavens. Have you forgotten what your light looks like? Let me remind you.

You burn with the oil of my presence as your fuel. In darkest nights, you shine ever brighter. Your love is not frail. It has been tested. Look at how far you've traveled on this road. Let's look through your history together, and let me show you the treasures that you have mined along the way. Can't you see it, the mark of my faithful love leading you in every twist of the road? Look at the growth of those seeds you have sown in tears. They are getting ready for harvest. The fruit of your life is so pleasing to taste. The incense of your devotion has a distinctly sweet fragrance. There is more beauty here than you imagined, yet even what you have experienced is but a foretaste of what is to come.

O Lord our God, let your sweet beauty rest upon us
and give us favor.
Come work with us, and then our works will endure,
and give us success in all we do.

PSALM 90:17

I never, ever leave.

I am with you today, beloved. Don't you know that it is a promise that stands the test of time? I never leave my beloved ones; no, I never abandon my own. Even when you're walking through the shadow of deep, dark valleys, I am present with you. I will not hide my love-light from you. I will draw you close with loving-kindness and comfort you with the cloak of my wraparound presence.

Even if you are completely alone in your life, with no friend or parent to turn to, I am with you. I am right here, right now, so pour out your heart before me. I am listening. Don't hold back. Just lay it all out there. Nothing you could say would ever push me away. I am here for keeps. My love for you is like a flowing fountain full of crystal-clear waters. Step in and find yourself refreshed. Nothing can talk me out of my delight in you. Even if just for a few moments, bask in the life-light of my joy today.

Even though the Lord may allow you
to go through a season of hardship and difficulty,
he himself will be there with you.
He will not hide himself from you.

ISAIAH 30:20

I am restoring your joy.

Do you sense the shift in seasons? You have entered the days of unrestricted joy. The tensions of yesterday have loosened. Your heart is blooming in the direction of love's light shining. The tender hopes are unfurling in the warmth of summer's long days. Where there was strain, it is now relaxing, and the tranquility and calm of long, quiet days are now upon you. The peace of perfect provision replaces the stress of never-enough. The struggle of staying at rest has passed. Refreshing is here, and there is no more striving. Lie back and enjoy the fruit of your restoration!

I have never stopped flowing over your life with unending streams of living water. You were never outside of my grip of grace. But here, your faith joins with the fruit of experience, and you are able to taste and see what you've been believing for. Let the joy of your fulfilled hopes flood your heart with thanksgiving. Leap and dance in the delight of my goodness. The oil of joy saturates your heart. Let it flow from your heart to your lips to your life!

Yes, he did mighty miracles and we are overjoyed!
Now, Lord, do it again! Restore us to our former glory!
May streams of your refreshing flow over us
until our dry hearts are drenched again.

Psalm 126:3–4

You will not be overtaken.

A s you follow the leadership of my love through the land-scape of your life, you will find that unexpected obstacles arise from time to time. But don't worry—I am with you. When enemies lie in wait to ambush you, don't be alarmed. I would never lead you into a trap. I see them from afar, and I am prepared to defend you. So do not be overcome by fear, for the cloak of my compassion already covers you.

You can trust that I will never abandon you to the whims of others. You are in my watchful care as long as you are living. Remember, I am the God who overcame the grave and demolished death. You were born again to a heavenly kingdom—my eternal realm. On this side of things, you will experience my deliverance over and over again. Take courage, my beloved, for I will never leave you. Let your heart find its confidence in my unfailing mercy that both leads you and follows behind you. You cannot escape my tender kindness, not even for a moment!

We can praise God over and over that he never left us!
God wouldn't allow the terror of our enemies to defeat us.

PSALM 124:6

Find your delight in me.

Lean in close and be filled with the fruit of the wisdom of my Word. There is endless delight in my presence, for I am the source of life itself. I know every hidden desire and every unspoken hope in your heart. When you look to me, you will inevitably find that I am the fulfillment of every longing. I will not hold back blessings from your life that benefit you, and I won't turn a deaf ear to your requests.

Trust me. Trust my timing. Even now, you have access to so much more than the blessings you have claimed. When you wait upon me, you will not be disappointed as I come through for you again and again. Let the tension of the in-between lead you into the abundance of my Spirit with you—right here, right now. There is more joy than you know what to do with, more delight in my heart than you can imagine. It may seem frivolous to you, when you have real needs in front of you, to seek after my delight. But I promise you, it is deep and full of lavish, loyal love that will wash over you, removing the dust of disappointment. Do you dare delve into this kind of delight today?

What delight comes to you when you wait upon the Lord!
For you will find what you long for.

MATTHEW 5:4

What I say goes.

In my love, you have been set free. Your life has been declared clean in the mercy-blood of Christ, and no one can contest it. What I have spoken is true. Who can come against you when I have declared you free in me? Who can overcome you when my love already has? No judgment can overrule my mercy. You are mine, child, and you will forever be!

Trust my wisdom above all others. Follow my lead like your life depends on it. Don't let flashy words distract you from the power of laid-down love. Look to me, and you will remain in the liberty of my loving-kindness, no matter what tries to enslave you. Shame is not a tactic I use to keep my children holy; you are holy because your life is hidden in me. Do not let fear trick you into thinking that you need to do something else to receive my favor. You are my child, and you are living in the delight of my kindness and favor simply because you belong to me. Align your life with my living Word, and you will never go astray.

The voice spoke to me again, saying,
"Nothing is unclean if God declares it to be clean."
ACTS 11:9

Let love lead you to wisdom.

Follow the way of love into the abundant wisdom found in my fellowship. Take hold of the nuggets of living truth that bring clarity to even the most confounding situations. I am full of perfect understanding, and when you look for my perception, I will not pull away or make it difficult for you. I long for you to live in the wisdom of my ways. It is simple, not mysterious.

You begin by doing what you already know to be true. Align in love's perfect ways. Mercy, compassion, and surrender are common characteristics found in my loyal lovers. You will have all the spiritual insight you need as you cultivate communion with me. Be quick to forgive and even quicker to seek forgiveness when you know you have hurt another. Revelation is not reserved for the super saints. Instead I offer it to all those who earnestly want to know me. And beloved, I know you. A desire for peace fills your heart. Come close now as I reveal more of my living knowledge to you.

I continue to pray for your love to grow and increase beyond measure, bringing you into the rich revelation of spiritual insight in all things.

PHILIPPIANS 1:9

July

Accept my kind of freedom.

Beloved, today you are living in the freedom of my wonderful love. Surrender every area that feels bound up by fear or lack of grace, and let my loving-kindness shine on you to remind you of the liberty of my law of love. There is no partial freedom in my kingdom. No, you are completely and wholly alive in my mercy!

My marvelous kindness and grave-robbing compassion touch every area of your life. Live in the light of this reality. Refuse to enter into old patterns and cycles that kept you stuck. Refuse to believe the lies of shame that say that failure is a death sentence. You have been born to life in my kingdom, and nothing can separate you from my resurrection power that sets every captive free. Walk in the glory of unhindered connection with your maker and Savior. I am restoring the areas of your heart that have been living under lies of shame. Yield to my love again today and find your joy here.

Let me be clear, the Anointed One has set us free—not partially, but completely and wonderfully free! We must always cherish this truth and stubbornly refuse to go back into the bondage of our past.

GALATIANS 5:1

I am your holy helper.

Daughter, what do you lack today? What is it that you need? I am your Good Shepherd, your loving leader, and your holy helper. Let me into your questions and your thoughts. Of course, I see them already, but I want this to be a conversation. I want the communion of fellowship with you. You will see my faithfulness more clearly when you voice what it is you want and you wait to hear my response. There is no need to hesitate here in my presence, though. I am patient, so you can take your time.

There is no situation that I am not equipped to handle. There is nothing you could say that would surprise me. You will find my mercy meets you every time. I am an understanding Father, and I invite you to lay down your built-up burdens today. You don't need to carry them any longer. I will give you the garment of my glory in its place. I offer comfort, not apathy. You will find no safer space than here with me. Let me in, daughter. Let me in, and I will offer what you need, for I have it in abundance.

The same God who made everything,
our Creator and our mighty maker,
he himself is our helper and defender!

PSALM 124:8

I don't change.

The same God who arranged the stars in the heavens is the God who revealed himself in flesh and bones through Jesus. I am the One who was, who is, and who is to come. I am Creator, I am Sustainer, and I am Redeemer. I am mighty and victorious. I am love embodied. I am the I AM. I never change, and I never will.

If you question my goodness, look at my character. I am faithful to my Word. I am consistent in kindness. In me there is fullness of glory. I never tire, never sleep, and never miss a thing. I don't ever leave my loyal lovers to rely on their own strength. In me is an abundance of grace, mercy, and power. I am never defeated. Even when it looked like death had won, I was victorious. I am the resurrection and the life, and I will be forever. I am the God of the humble. I am your God, and you belong to me. I will never lead you where I have not already gone. Bind your heart to mine, and I will always lead you in loyal love.

Jesus, the Anointed One, is always the same—
yesterday, today, and forever.

HEBREWS 13:8

You are free.

B eloved, I am surrounding you with my very present peace today. Lavish love has set you free, so live as one who has been released from every chain. There is no darkness that I haven't already overcome with the glorious light of my salvation. Nothing could keep you stuck in the cycles of shame anymore. I have lifted every curse, broken every shackle, and opened every locked door that darkness used to keep you small and afraid.

I am leading you into joy unspeakable, beloved, so follow me. There's no need to stay in the comfort of your pain anymore. I have ministered healing, and I am leading you into deeper recovery. Know that you can trust me with your heart. I will not fail you. Let your feet find their course as they run into the delight of my pure affection. Nothing holds you back except for your own hesitation. Take my hand and put all your trust in me. I am better than your wildest expectations and hopes. You were made to be abundantly free in me, so throw off your inhibitions and be wholly unrestricted in my love today!

He sent me to heal the wounds of the brokenhearted,
to tell captives, "You are free,"
and to tell prisoners, "Be free from your darkness."

ISAIAH 61:1

I fight for you.

I am your great defender, and you can always count on me to fight for you. There's no need to rush to the frontline of your battles, swinging with all you've got. Trust me, I know how to turn the tide of every battle so that it works out in the best possible way. Rely on me, for I know what I'm doing. I am your champion defender in every trouble. Though you cannot escape trials, you can trust that I will lead you faithfully through each and every one.

My insights are pure, and my wisdom takes everything into account. There's no need to let worries overtake your senses, for I am more than capable. The discomfort of the unknown is a purely human experience, for I see all—every possible outcome. Trust my higher perspective that leads you in love and keeps you from needless harm. I am working on your behalf, so you can rest in the confidence of my faithful leadership over your life.

> His wrap-around presence always protects me.
> For he is my champion defender;
> there's no risk of failure with God.
> So why would I let worry paralyze me,
> even when troubles multiply around me?
>
> PSALM 62:2

Embrace my truth.

Beloved, let your heart open up to the loving correction of my wisdom at work in your life. Think about it like this: You and I are walking the winding path of your life, hand in hand. When you stop for a moment too long or start to wander off the safety of the path, my gentle hand nudges you on and pulls you back onto the pathway of peace. My truth is like that—tender and full of clear insight. I see where we are going, and I know the dangers behind, around, and ahead. Will you let my love direct you? My intentions for you are always for your best.

My character doesn't change. That's really good news. I am faithful, and there's no chance of ever getting yourself into a situation that I won't help you through. I never, ever leave. However, there is freedom of choice for you. I promise that I will not ever drag you along or force a decision upon you. But know that choosing to live your life surrendered to my leadership means allowing your heart to trust that my loving wisdom knows the best routes and the most advantageous pursuits for you. As you align your life with my loving light, you will find that even the thorniest branches produce beautiful roses. Nothing can escape my redemptive power—not any area of your life, past, present, or future!

If you embrace the truth,
it will release more freedom into your lives.

JOHN 8:32

Choose wisely.

I n my love, you have found freedom to rise to your true identity. Tune into my compassion, which is so strong that my very heart beats with the truth of who I created you to be. I have called you my own, and I am a good Father with a heart full of delight over you. When you learn and grow and find your feet beneath you, it fills me with pride. Don't stop taking risks in love and life as you follow the wisdom of my Word.

I am not demanding. You are free to choose how you will live. Even in surrender, you could go a variety of ways. You could take multiple expressions in your life that align with my mercy. Whatever you decide to do, be sure that it is actually a fruit of your freedom. In other words, do not link your life with something that enslaves you. The blood of the Lamb has set you free from everything that hinders love, so don't go the way of indentured servitude. Don't believe the lies of temporary pleasure and quick returns, for they are a trap. Why be bound by chains again when you are reborn to live unencumbered? But even if you find yourself bound up, look to me, and I will lead you into freedom again.

It's true that our freedom allows us to do anything,
but that doesn't mean that everything we do is good for us.
I'm free to do as I choose,
but I choose to never be enslaved to anything.

1 CORINTHIANS 6:12

I am your breakthrough.

In every area where you cannot see a way out, I am your breakthrough. I will never leave you to be overtaken by fear or trauma. I am your way-maker, your bright and guiding light, your saving grace, and your holy help at every turn. I never tire of giving you help when you are stuck. Why try to break free on your own, with your limited resources and solutions, when you have a good and faithful Father caring for you?

Today is the day of your glorious hope rising as I come through for you again. What areas of your life need my powerful touch? Don't hold back a single one. Watch and see how I release peace in your soul while I rise up as your defense, your Advocate, and your victory. Remind yourself of my faithfulness. Do you think I will fail you now? Joy will bubble up once more as you witness my miracle-working power in your life. I am God of the now, present in every moment with an abundance of mercy. Be filled again and again with the rich fruit of my presence!

A new song for a new day rises up in me
every time I think about how he breaks through for me!
Ecstatic praise pours out of my mouth until
everyone hears how God has set me free.

PSALM 40:3

Spread the word.

C an you see how my faithful love has changed your life? Think about this and let the joy of my presence flood your being. The testimony of fulfilled longings is a taste of who I am and what I do. Don't you see how good I am? Let your heart fill with the wonder of a child marveling at things that are too great to understand. The mystery of my Spirit-life alive in you is waiting for your attention today. Consider the works of my hands and how all of creation echoes my goodness. Search out the stamps of my kindness around you. I promise you won't have to look hard.

It's time to look through the lens of my higher perspective once again. The ways of this world would have you forget my sovereignty and how I mark even the most defiled things with my mercy and make them new in me. I bring rebirth from destruction and defeat. Let heaven's outlook influence your own as you look for evidence of my life-giving mercy. You will find it. Just as you need this reminder of good news that is living and active, so do others. Spread the word, and watch as peace opens its wide wings over the chaos and settles the uncertainties of doubt and fear.

Unable to contain themselves,
they went out and spread the news everywhere!

MATTHEW 9:31

I will deliver you.

Taste and see the sweetness of my love, daughter. The kindness of my kingdom will restore every loss you experience. You will encounter my miracle-deliverance whenever your plans fall apart and your strategies get shot down. Lean on me and my wisdom. I surely will not let you down. I will strengthen you no matter how frail you feel. Let my power work out your victory as you drink from my spring of delight. Do not underestimate the power of joy in the face of unfavorable odds. Surely nothing will take you out, and fear will not overcome you. I am your liberator and your great deliverer.

As my beloved child, you are wrapped up in the covering of my constant compassion all the days of your life. There is not a circumstance or a split-second when I am not present to you. I am here with you. I will lead you out of every trial with my kindness dripping off of you like the oil of Aaron's beard.

Some find their strength in their weapons and wisdom,
but my miracle deliverance can never be won by men.
Our boast is in the Lord our God,
who makes us strong and gives us victory!

PSALM 20:7

Liberty is yours.

In my love, you are free to be, free to dance, free to weep, and free to shout for joy. There is nothing off-limits for you. You are fully accepted as my own, and as such, you have unlimited access to my presence. I surround you with my wraparound love at all times. When you feel hemmed in by limiting circumstances, look to me and ask for my perspective. I will never fail to provide the wisdom of truth that sets your heart free, even in surrender.

Do not be deceived by the letter of the laws of this world that says you have limited freedoms. In my kingdom, there is a higher principle at work: the law of love. You are free to choose what you will, as long as you are not choosing enslavement. Beware the enticing offers of quick-returns and self-pleasures. They may satisfy for a moment, but they will leave you more deficient than you were at first. Be loyal to love's liberty, and you will never be put to shame. Throw off the shackles that I have already broken and walk in the light of my love that truly satisfies the desires of your heart.

Those who set their gaze deeply into the perfecting law of liberty are fascinated by and respond to the truth they hear and are strengthened by it—they experience God's blessing in all that they do!

JAMES 1:25

I always triumph.

B ind your life to mine, the miracle maker and all-sufficient One. I will never let you down. In the time of testing and of trial, I will always lead you out in triumph—every single time. I am the God of redemption, of renewal, and of resurrection. What you see as an end, I see as an opportunity. I am full of power and might. I am known as the miracle-working God. I am God of the impossible, for nothing is unattainable for me.

Lean into my loyal love today and be reminded of the great power of my mercy that sets every captive free. Where you are stuck, I am breaking down walls. Take my hand and follow me into your freedom—dance into the light of my glorious presence. You will find completeness in the fullness of my love. There is no shadow here, nothing that can keep you hidden. Come alive in the light of my life. Rise up and let out a shout of faith. Kindness covers you all the days of your life!

Look! Here comes Lord Yahweh as a victorious warrior;
he triumphs with his awesome power.
Watch as he brings with him his reward
and the spoils of victory to give *to his people.*

ISAIAH 40:10

Confidence grows in my peace.

D raw near to my heart in the fellowship of my Spirit, beloved. I am close, and I am full of love to lavish on you. Let the wisdom that has instructed you in my constant character lead you deeper into the peace of my presence. You have the serenity of my Spirit like a bubbling fountain alive within you. Drink of the pure waters of my living love. Rest here and find that every worry floats off on the breeze of my faithful care.

The roots of your confidence are growing deep in the soil of my faithful love. You are growing into a strong and mighty oak, unshakable in the storms of life. Do not worry when the winds of testing come, for you have firmly planted roots. My peace is your plentiful portion in every season of the soul. Whenever you are lacking, run into my presence and find the refreshing reminders of my faithfulness that will quell the fears that arise. I remain unchanging in mercy and unfailing in saving grace. Let your heart be reminded that I never fail!

Everything I've taught you is so that the peace which is in me will be in you and will give you great confidence as you rest in me.

JOHN 16:33

Hope is never far.

Fix your eyes on me in your joys and in your pain. I am celebrating with you in your victories and comforting you in your disappointments. Come to me when you are weary and burdened. I will give you rest. I hear the cries of your heart even when they don't reach your lips. I see every hidden regret and frustration. I see the pain that setbacks have caused you. But child, I am still with you, and I am making all things new.

Watch what my love can do as I restore to you the joy of your salvation. Hope that seemed impractical even moments ago is now within reach. Don't you know that I never stop rescuing my beloved ones? You cannot sink into a pit where I cannot reach you. Even now, my love-light is shining on you. I am closer than you realize, working in ways you have yet to recognize. Don't fear abandonment. I never, ever forsake my own, and you belong to me. I surround you with songs of deliverance when you cannot see a way out of your troubles. I am behind and before you, leading you into the joy of my freedom.

Lord, you know and understand all the hopes of the humble
and will hear their cries and comfort their hearts,
helping them all!

PSALM 10:17

My light of life shines on you.

You are living in the light of my glorious presence. Just as the noonday sun brightly covers all that is in its path, so does my love reach you. Turn to me like a flower does the sun; open up in love's light. My radiance removes every shadow, so let your heart open as I pour my favor out over you. Your love is my delight. I cannot express the depths of my delight over your life. The smile on your face, the glisten in your eyes—it brings a twinkle to my own!

My glory is streaming from my throne where I keep a watchful eye on all that is going on in the world. You cannot escape the rays of my loyal love that cover the earth and everything in it. Come alive in my presence that nestles around you. I am so very near. Breathe in the peace of my Spirit. Drink up the refreshing waters of my kindness. Eat of my rich wisdom. Fellowship with the light, and you will never need to question the motives of darkness, for your own life is found in my favor.

Life-giving light streams from the presence of a king,
and his favor is showered upon those who please him.

PROVERBS 16:15

Take my hand in yours.

Beloved, every desire of your heart is as clear as day to me. I note each one, and I will not let your longings remain unfulfilled. Trust me to be the satisfier and the source, even when you don't understand my ways. I see the progression of every well-laid plan and of every short-lived endeavor. Will you trust me to guide you?

Place your hand in mine as I lead you into my glory. I offer you all the wisdom you'll ever need, and I will keep you safe in the midst of every storm we encounter. Though some will quiet with my powerful presence, others will require you to stay hidden in my cloak, pulled to my side. I will always rescue you when you need it, for I am an ever-present help in time of trouble. Do not fear when the skies darken and the rumbling of thunder rolls your way. I will teach you to stay in my perfect peace, and I will fulfill your longings along the way with my abundant provision. Trust me and stay close, and I will guide you every step of the way.

Escort me along the way; take me by the hand and teach me.
For you are the God of my increasing salvation;
I have wrapped my heart into yours!

PSALM 25:5

Leave your worries with me.

I am the God of your abundant provision and your comfort in every trouble. There is nothing you need that I will not provide you. Look at the world around you. Do you see the birds and how they always have food when they need it? Wild animals do not lack what they need to survive, and neither do you. I take close care of you.

Do not give over to worries about what you will eat or drink when your supplies run short. From my hand of abundance, you will have all you need and more. There will be times when you're getting by with less than you may be accustomed to, but lean into my grace even more. Less is not the same as not enough. Let your heart be full of trust as I provide for all of your needs. Let your eyes see through the lens of my perception, full of truth. Leave all your worries here with me since they're a needless burden to bear. My faithfulness is your guard, so let my loyal love strengthen you as you release every fear into my capable hands.

This is why I tell you to never be worried about your life, for all that you need will be provided, such as food, water, clothing—everything your body needs.

MATTHEW 6:25

I am a springing well.

I am a well of living water to refresh and satisfy all who draw from my life-giving presence. My fountain of joy and delight never diminishes. I am an overflowing fountain of pure goodness. Today is the day to find yourself refreshed in the springs of my mercy. I never run dry, so there's no need for you to regulate your access to my love. I want you to live in the pure pool of my kindness. Don't ration yourself when I have given you the freedom to drink deeply at all times.

Be revived in my joy today and come alive in my delight. You will flourish like a well-cared-for garden as my Spirit-life continually refreshes you. Even the most arid conditions will become like an oasis as you drink freely of my love. I am your source. Here, in this place of unhindered fellowship, let your roots go deep in the soil of my affection. Watch as my favor transforms the dry and barren parts into lush gardens of grace. What a beautiful fragrance is your surrendered life to my senses. Keep leaning in, love. It only gets better from here!

Yahweh…will fill you with refreshment
even when you are in a dry, difficult place.
He will continually restore strength to you,
so you will flourish like a well-watered garden
and like an ever-flowing, trustworthy spring of blessing.

ISAIAH 58:11

Relax, beloved.

Finding true rest is as simple as trust, beloved. Don't over-complicate it. You don't need to accomplish one more thing to earn your right to rest. I have covered you with my kindness. My offer to you is more than you could accomplish on your own, so there is no need to strive for my favor. I've already freely offered it to you. You are living in its light. Don't let fear disguised as worry turn rest into a reward. It is my gift to you!

Let the confidence of my love surround you with peace in my Spirit. There will always be more to do when you're living according to the world's ways. Align your life with mine and allow yourself the gift of rest without guilt. There is no reason to push yourself to the bone when I am already at work on your behalf. You are not toiling without an end in sight if you let your life reflect my own. There is purpose in rest. There is refreshment in enjoying what you have, here and now, without quickly moving on to the next thing. Trust me, beloved. I've got you. Now, relax.

Now I can say to myself and to all,
"Relax and rest, be confident and serene,
for the Lord rewards fully those who simply trust in him."
PSALM 116:7

I am bringing you back.

B eloved, I have been with you in the pain, weeping with you and comforting you with the peace of my presence. I never delight in the sorrows of your soul, and I don't diminish the grief that tears at your heart. I am acquainted with your suffering, child. Even so, put your trust in me. Follow my loving leading as I guide you into my goodness. I am bringing you back to life and restoring what loss took from you.

Lean into my kindness, and let my mercy uphold you when you have no strength of your own. I am carrying you into your renewal. With joy, I bring you into a new day. Revival is upon you. You will run again with passion, set free to dance upon every disappointment. There will be no holding you back from the delight of your destiny, for it is already written. Take hope, beloved, for I am still knitting the thread of redemption love through every detail of your story. What I put in place, no one can remove!

See if there is any path of pain I'm walking on,
and lead me back to your glorious, everlasting ways—
the path that brings me back to you.

PSALM 139:24

Walk in righteousness.

When you walk in the way of love, every step you take is holy. Every surrender, every humble choice to serve another, every conscious act of trust—it is all a reflection of my life at work in you. Look at the fruit of your life and not just on the surface. You will find my Spirit's fruit in a myriad of life-giving ways. It is evident in the attitude of hopeful trust, and it is clear in your willingness to offer mercy toward yourself and others when hurts are sown. Spirit-life is growing in you when you continually turn toward me and when you rely more on my goodness than your own.

Keep walking the pathways of my kindness. Promote peace, celebrate in the joys of others, offer comfort to those who are grieving, and continue to choose mercy over judgment. Keep doing the good that is already at work in your life. Don't abandon the hope that has fueled your dreams and has kept your heart openly feeding on my faithfulness. Continually turn your attention toward me and feast on the confidence of my unfailing love!

We pray that you would walk in the ways of true righteousness, pleasing God in every good thing you do. Then you'll become fruit-bearing branches, yielding to his life, and maturing in the rich experience of knowing God in his fullness!

COLOSSIANS 1:10

Build on the foundation of faith.

Your life has been established upon the foundation of my faithfulness. From the rising of the sun to its setting, I am faithfully working out my promises in your life. You can build upon the solid rock of my goodness by joining your heart with mine in open communion. When you don't know what to do, pray. When you don't know what to say, open your heart all the same. I read you like a book, and I know even better than you do what you need in every moment.

Choosing to continually turn your attention to me will build a greater capacity within you to believe me for all that I say I will do. It will train your eyes to spot my tangible goodness. It's not that I am more faithful when you're paying attention; it's just that you will be able to spot it more easily. Today join with my Spirit as you lift up your own in a continual conversation. You will see my goodness in the land of the living as you constantly commune with me.

You, my delightfully loved friends, constantly and progressively
build yourselves up on the foundation of your most holy faith
by praying every moment in the Spirit.

JUDE 20

My love is not selfish.

B eloved, take note today of the pure, untainted nature of my affection. It is not dependent on any outside force. It is the driving force of all I do, for it is my life force. Love is who I am. My love is generous, selflessly offering pure kindness to all. Yielding love saturates my mercy. It does not take account of self-serving purposes. It is always flowing out like a rushing river. It does not require reciprocation. It has no reservations, and there are no hindrances to its power.

In the same way that you receive from this endless flow of loving-kindness, so learn to love others. Then you will be reflecting the kind of God I am to all those you come into contact with. If what you're doing is for your own sake alone, I tell you—search your motives and lay them down in surrender. When you model your life after Christ, you will live as a shining beacon of light. Let your marvelous freedom lead you into deeper joy as you lay down your own preferences in favor of my righteous wisdom.

Beloved ones, God has called us to live a life of freedom in the Holy Spirit. ... Freedom means that we become so completely free of self-indulgence that we become servants of one another, expressing love in all we do.

GALATIANS 5:13

JULY 24

Aspire to peace.

L et the serenity of my presence fill your soul today. Look to me, beloved, for I have not gone anywhere. I have sown the seeds of my peace in your heart, and they will blossom and bear fruit. Take the bounty that is within you and sow into those around you. Be a promoter of my perfect peace in every situation. The harmony you cultivate within your own fields of opportunity does not diminish my justice.

Whatever you put your hand to, do it with the grace of my love that empowers you to do it well. Do not sow seeds of doubt and contention, and do not participate with those who do. Make yourself at home in the rest of my perfect peace, and do not partner with anything that stirs fear and dissension. Your life will be fruitful when you live in the light of my glorious life. There is no shadow in my love; you won't find a single hurtful motivation in its depths. Drink deeply of the purity of my presence, and you will always have something uplifting to offer others. You are a child of the light, so live in my light, shining brightly for all to see.

Aspire to lead a calm and peaceful life as you mind your own business and earn your living, just as we've taught you.

1 THESSALONIANS 4:11

I am your faithful friend.

I am the One who sticks closer than a sister. I am more dependable than a devoted mother. I walk with you through every situation, always lending a listening ear when you need it. I am there to support you in every endeavor, always willing to lend a helping hand. I offer you the sagest advice in your difficulties. I never turn away from you in your dark days. I love you for who you are, never expecting you to put on a show or be picture-perfect.

I know you at your best and at your worst, and my affection for you never wavers. Why look for satisfaction in others' perceptions of you when you already have full acceptance with me? I love you the same in your most vulnerable state as I do when you are at the top of your game. Your worth does not come from what you offer me. Rather it is in who I say that you are—and you are mine. Lay it all out there with me in every moment. I always want you to share openly with me. I won't ever withhold my companionship from you, so find your joy and comfort here in this exchange, as I do with you.

The Lord sees all we do; he watches over his friends day and night.
His godly ones receive the answers they seek whenever they
cry out to him.

PSALM 34:15

My grace will transform you.

B eloved, I am offering you the fullness of my grace today. Let it wash over you, filling every dry and weary crack in your armor. Let it empower you with my limitless strength in place of your worn-out weakness. This is a brand-new opportunity to receive my glorious mercy-might. There's never been a moment like now. Embrace the present and open up to my life-giving presence.

Let the glory of my pure affection flood your thoughts. I am your good and present God. I am your source, and I am the One who purifies you. I am leading you into greater glory as you follow my ways. In the fellowship of my Spirit, you are coming alive. Let today be the day of your overwhelming joy. You are mine. You are becoming more like me as you gaze into my beauty. I will pour over you the revelation of my truth in new ways as you seek me. Let the good fruit of my life in you ripen in your heart as you continue to soak in my goodness. Let love arise, and with it, pure delight in this marvelous exchange.

It was only through this wonderful grace that we believed in him. Nothing we did could ever earn this salvation, for it was the gracious gift from God that brought us to Christ!

EPHESIANS 2:8

You are united with me.

My child, let your confidence grow today as you revel in the understanding that you are mine and I am yours. You have open access to my heart whenever you seek it. Turn your attention to me, and you will find that I am always attentive. I have so much to share with you—not only the treasures of wisdom that will produce bountiful fruit in your life but also the lavish love of my affection that never runs out or runs dry!

Let my grace be the strength that fills you when you have nothing left to give. There is no need to struggle in your own limited might when you have my free-flowing power to draw from. I have enough to cover every weakness, so don't you worry about it. Will you venture deeper into my heart today as I lead you into the garden of my goodness? Let's not waste this moment. Grab hold of it and offer me your undivided attention. You will not regret it.

Live your life empowered by God's free-flowing grace,
which is your true strength,
found in the anointing of Jesus and your union with him!
2 TIMOTHY 2:1

Stay awake.

Today is the day of your awakened hope. Let it rise up within you and bring light to my revelation-knowledge. In your life, you will face trials, but you will also experience my mighty power and miracles as you wait upon me. Take hope and be courageous, for I am with you. Don't grow lazy in love, forgetting the purpose of connection. You are an overcomer, daughter. Fill up on my love. It is meant to both sustain and propel you. Whatever you do, do not lose sight of me. I am mighty and able, and I am working out my goodness in your life—even when you cannot see it.

Let your heart grow strong in my mercy, holding on to the promises of my faithful Word. You are not alone in anything you face, and there is nothing that comes across your path that is a mystery to me. If all you can do is hold on—then, my dear, do it. I have got you, and nothing can loosen the grip of grace I have over your life. No one can take you from my grasp. Let your faith be fastened to my faithfulness.

Remember to stay alert and hold firmly to all that you believe.
Be mighty and full of courage.

1 CORINTHIANS 16:13

Your freedom can set others free.

I n the light of your freedom, you set others free. Be sure to remember to line your choices with loyal love. The liberty in which you live your life will offend some while inspiring others. If you want to promote love and peace, make sure to consider your influence in others' lives. Let your heart be full of my delight that celebrates in others' freedom as well as your own.

There is no need to live for yourself. Have you not already found joy in the laying down of your life to my will and ways? Your surrender has led you to ultimate freedom. As children grow in understanding, they begin to shift from focusing on themselves to an awareness of how their words and actions affect others around them. Will you let your own understanding deepen as you consider others as much as you consider your own liberties? This is a chance for you to grow up in my love a little. Let your love mature, beloved, as you follow my example.

Follow my example, for I try to please everyone in all things, rather than putting my liberty first. I sincerely attempt to do anything I can so that others may be saved.

1 CORINTHIANS 10:33

Hope is not lost.

B eloved, you have everything you need to live a life that is pleasing to me and fulfilling for you. When you lay down your life for my sake, letting love take the lead in every situation, you will find that there is more satisfaction in surrender than in self-fulfilled dreams. I will satisfy every longing with the refreshing waters of my living-love through my Spirit. Trust me. I know what I'm doing.

Continue to cultivate the open connection of communion with me through unceasing prayer. There is not a single moment where your voice goes unheard. The richness of our relationship will only grow as you continually turn to me. It is easy to find delight on the bright and sunny days this life offers, but don't forget that my love is just as pure and rich when you're in the midst of a raging storm. Do not give up hope, for my persistent help is always yours. The sun will break through, and joy will burst forth once more. So keep praying, keep seeking me, and don't lose sight of the hope you have in me.

One day Jesus taught the apostles to keep praying
and never stop or lose hope.

LUKE 18:1

Your faith releases my power.

When you exercise your faith in my faithful presence, you will see my power at work in your life. When you are alive in the knowledge of my resources as your own, cultivating your confidence and practicing its implications, you are growing up in your faith. To believe something and not test it out is akin to foolishness. Let your belief play out in real time. Take me at my Word by pressing into what I have offered you in it.

My faithfulness does not depend upon your faith, for nothing can deter me from what I said I would do. However you have more authority than you have been living. You are a child of God with the Holy Spirit alive inside of you. Do not let fear of disappointment keep you from pressing into the abundance of my kingdom. I will release my power through you as you align your life and words with my unfailing character. Be like Peter who walked on the water with his eyes fixed on me. Nothing is impossible for anyone who believes.

Jesus responded, "If you have even the smallest measure of authentic faith, it would be powerful enough to say to this large tree, 'My faith will pull you up by the roots and throw you into the sea,' and it will respond to your faith and obey you."

LUKE 17:6

August

My joy is yours.

Daughter, come alive in my presence today. There is fullness of joy here—an abundance of delight. There is no lack of pure affection in my heart toward you. You will find that your own well of joy fills to overflowing as you drink in the plenty of my pleasure over you. My desire for you is that you know how completely I love you. You are fully accepted, dripping in my loving-kindness.

My pure pleasure is not even a little dependent on what you have to offer me. Don't get me wrong, every time you surrender yourself in laid-down love, it moves my heart with pride. But it can never add to the measure of my love for you because my love is always and forever overflowing. I love you because it is my nature to love. I delight in you, my beloved daughter. My kindness covers you all the days of your life. Today is no different. Drink it in! My love that seems too good to be true is pouring over you.

We are writing these things to you because we want to release to you our fullness of joy.

1 JOHN 1:4

There is no shadow of turning.

C ome close, beloved, and see that I am right here. You don't have to search hard for my presence. I am already with you. Let your heart be encouraged in my constant compassion today. I am light, and in me all is clear. Even now, let me bring revelation to your understanding of my nearness.

You have heard it said that there is no shadow of turning in me. It is true, child, for I never turn to leave. I am constant and true, and I never abandon my beloved ones. You can count on my consistent care and presence. Though others come and go from your life at various times, you can count on me. I never, ever leave. I am never distracted. Your life is like an open book before me, and I see every detail clearly. Trust my faithfulness, for I will not fail you. I have never left any of my loyal lovers, and I'm not about to start now. Here I am, right with you—right where I can always be found.

This is the life-giving message we heard him share and it's still ringing in our ears. We now repeat his words to you: God is pure light. You will never find even a trace of darkness in him.

1 JOHN 1:5

Find wisdom in patience.

Lean in close as I share my kingdom principles with you. Tune your ears to the frequency of my heart even when others are speaking. If you will listen with ears to hear, you will have insight into what is behind people's words. Don't listen just to formulate a reply. Instead hear with ears that carefully consider the weight of another's experience. Compassion is a reliable tool in every circumstance. Beloved one, you reflect me well when you let kindness line your conscious choices.

Practice patience in all things, looking to me for your cues. Let me instruct you in my holy wisdom, whether you're in the waiting or ready to move ahead. When you are angry, turn to me and receive my mercy that cools even the hottest temper. Wait until you are full of my righteous peace before you move on in your purpose so that you will not lead others to associate my name with your rage. And when you do boil over, be quick to seek forgiveness and repent. Let your heart remain humble without making excuses for your behavior. My loyal love is the royal robe of your identity. Allow me to wrap it around you as you step outside of old patterns and into my glorious freedom.

Take this to heart: Be quick to listen, but slow to speak. And be slow to become angry, for human anger is never a legitimate tool to promote God's righteous purpose.

JAMES 1:19–20

Focus on today.

I see your cares and the burdens you've been carrying, child. Let me lift your worries today. There's no need for you to buckle under their weight. You don't need to keep track of the concerns that the uncertainty of tomorrow may bring. Trust me. Though you don't know how things will play out, I always do. You can trust me to guide you through it all. Let me lead you in love on my pathway of peace.

Today focus only on what is in front of you. Put your energy where you are, in the present moment. You cannot control tomorrow, but you can take hold of what is in front of you today. Cast your anxieties into my sea of mercy and believe that I can handle them all. Find the peace in the present as you trust me for everything you cannot yet see. With my grace to strengthen you, you have everything you need for the right here and right now.

Refuse to worry about tomorrow, but deal with each challenge that comes your way, one day at a time. Tomorrow will take care of itself.
MATTHEW 6:34

Let passion fuel you.

B eloved, on the journey of this life, you have a multitude of opportunities to decide what you will let fuel you. In my heart of lavish love is abundance for all that you could ever need. Every day is a new opportunity for you to receive fresh grace and new mercies. Drink from my pool of plenty. Let my wraparound presence build you up in compassion today. Your lack could never exceed the limits of my love, for there are none. In fact, the greater the deficiency you feel, the more room you have for my power to fill you up and move in your life.

Take heart today, child, that I am your source and your strength. The passion of my heart will fill yours as you run into my presence time after time. Let my copious kindness reinforce the walls of your purpose as you find that every answer you are looking for is in my boundless love. Fill up on my mercy now. It is right here for you to simply receive!

I admit that I haven't yet acquired the absolute fullness that I'm pursuing, but I run with passion into his abundance so that I may reach the purpose that Jesus Christ has called me to fulfill and wants me to discover.

PHILIPPIANS 3:12

Don't stop meeting together.

I n these days of busyness, don't let the peace of my wisdom escape you. I created you for fellowship in me and with others. After I made Adam, I did not stop creating for a reason. It is good for you to have flesh and blood family to experience the beauty of community. I never meant for you to be alone. Let the bond of love keep you meeting together with others—especially those who walk in my ways.

You will find encouragement in the shared experiences of my beloved ones. You will find comfort with those who have mourned, and you will have joy when you celebrate with others. You are like iron sharpening iron, building each other up in faith. Trust me; your heart will find courage and love in the communion of common saints. It gives you opportunity to practice mercy through forgiveness, faith through prayer and expectation, and kindness through service. In the fellowship of faith, you will grow strong, for a cord of three strands cannot be easily broken.

This means that when we come together and are side by side,
something wonderful will be released.
We can expect to be co-encouraged
and co-comforted by each other's faith!

ROMANS 1:12

Let this be your holy pursuit.

Run into my arms of grace again today as you find the refreshment your soul longs for. Leave behind all the pursuits that drain you of the passion of your purpose. Come, be aligned in my love, and let the questions you have become clear in the peace of my wisdom. The plumb line of my mercy will make your choices clearer. As you throw off everything that hinders love, you will find that your path of pursuit smooths before you.

Follow along the pathway of my peace, and you will not be disappointed in the end. The power of a focused life is the purity of purpose. Spend your energy on the building up of your faith and take your time with that which deepens your love for me and for others. Dig into the wisdom of my Word, and project my promises onto the screen of your heart. Hide yourself in my faithfulness as you delight yourself in the affections of my heart. You cannot go wrong when you build your life upon the rock of my mercy. Keep building on the framework of holiness, beloved. It will be worth it!

Run as fast as you can from all the ambitions and lusts of youth; and chase after all that is pure. Whatever builds up your faith and deepens your love must become your holy pursuit.

2 TIMOTHY 2:22

I am your goodness.

Y ou could search the entire earth for something to satisfy your soul, but you would never find a better love than mine. Let every longing lead you back to me, for I will satisfy each one. I will lavish over you my loyal love that sets you free from every hindrance and causes your soul to come alive. Let your desires lead you to my holy place, where I share the wonders of my wisdom with my beloved ones. Let joy fill your heart as you enter in, unhindered and unashamed!

It's a day to celebrate. You are welcome, as always, with open arms to my table of plenty. Feast on my goodness again. I do not serve stale, day-old bread. Before you is a banquet of delight, full of the fruits of my kingdom. Eat the delicacy of my kindness and drink the sweetness of my compassion. There is so much available to you at all times. Don't hesitate, even if you don't think you need anything. Come and enjoy yourself in my company. I would love nothing more!

Celebrate the goodness of God!
He shows this kindness to everyone who is his.
Go ahead—shout for joy,
all you upright ones who want to please him!
Psalm 32:11

AUGUST 9

I am alive.

B eloved, let your heart take hope in my resurrection power today. I am more than able to redeem every broken dream, shot-down expectation, and pressed-down plan. My ways are so much better than your own, for they take into account the whole picture, every single time. Though disappointment will not escape your human experience, I will never fail you. I am living and active in your life. I am the God who raises up those that death has stolen and awakens them to abundant, everlasting life.

Trust me when your heart starts to waver. Bind your hope to my faithfulness. I am not dead, and I am not distant. My life is yours now. You have been born again into an eternal kingdom full of light and glory-filled existence. My resurrection power is the same force at work within you. That's right, you have the Holy Spirit as a kiss of my promised presence that never abandons you. Let the strength of my loyal love flood you—body, soul, and mind—as you open up to receive more of my living understanding. You will see signs and experience wonders as you walk in the light of my life.

Jesus proved to them with many convincing signs that he had been resurrected. During these encounters, he taught them the truths of God's kingdom realm.

ACTS 1:3

Follow me to be refreshed.

Daughter, are you weary? Does your heart long for refreshing, but the pull of the weight of the world drags you down? Look to me. Let me lead you to the resting place of my love where I will pour over you my living waters of mercy. I will revive you as you rest in me and drink deeply of my presence.

There is no need to carry around with you the burdens of weighty matters like they are badges of honor. I am the lifter of your head, so look into my eyes now. Don't you see that I can handle all your baggage? I care for you, and I offer you the peace that you've been longing for. Rest awhile in my presence that demands nothing from you. Receive my lavish love. Be filled with my life-giving Spirit that provides everything you need in every moment. I am the master restorer, making all things new—including you. Let your heart find relief in the exchange of your heaviness for my delight.

I will pour refreshing water on the thirsty and streams on the dry ground. I will pour out my Spirit on your children, my blessing upon your descendants.

ISAIAH 44:3

Harvest is coming.

Beloved, be encouraged today. For every seed sown in tears, there is an abundant return on its way. When you walked through the valley of suffering and your resolve wavered, my grace covered your steps with the fertilizer of my redemption. I held you up when you had no strength of your own. Leaning on me was your strength, not your weakness. You will see now, as you look back, that there is a lush garden where once there was a dry desert.

You cannot imagine the sweet abundance of my blessing that is coming to you. There will be restoration for loss and redemption for destruction. Get ready for the goodness by preparing your heart. I have already enlarged your capacity as you've chosen to trust me. Look with eyes of faith over our history. Stir up memories of promises fulfilled, for there is more coming. Let your expectation grow as you consider the works of my hands and my trustworthy leadership. Even if you still can't see the treasures that were hidden in the darkness, know that they are there. You will be in awe when you see all that I've done for you!

They may weep as they go out carrying their seed to sow,
but they will return with joyful laughter and shouting with gladness
as they bring back armloads of blessing and a harvest overflowing!

PSALM 126:6

Your gifts matter.

You have been called by name, child, and you are mine. You are uniquely talented, and you are a vibrant gift to the family of my beloved ones. When you first awakened to love's call in your life, there was so much rapid growth as you depended on both me and my loyal lovers to teach you my kingdom ways. You developed quickly in the nurturing and wisdom of my love. You heeded the teachings of those who aligned their lives with mine, and you sought to be like them. Do not diminish the value of this time, for it set you up to continually seek me.

Do not forget the gifts that you received in the early days of your learning. They are still at work in your life. Practice them and use them for the benefit of others. No one else can offer what you do in the way you do it. Do not be convinced that another could fill your spot, for there is only one you. Let your light shine brightly as you live in the confidence of who I have created you to be. Use what you've received, and you will receive more. There is no shortage in me. Let love propel you, beloved.

Don't minimize the powerful gift that operates in your life, for it was imparted to you by the laying on of hands of the elders and was activated through the prophecy they spoke over you.

1 TIMOTHY 4:14

I keep every promise.

Y ou will feast on my faithfulness as I fulfill every promise that I have spoken. When the winds of testing come, do not lose hope. The protection of my presence hides you. I will keep you safe so that not a single bit of my goodness will be lost. For even in destruction, I rebuild and restore. I make all things new. Trust me, for I always lead you in love. I am constant and true.

Fix your heart on me, and set your eyes on my trustworthy character. Even if you were to forget my promises, I never will. I am unchanging in loyal love and magnanimous mercy. I see every detail that you overlook. When you think you know better than I do, lean into my wisdom. I will share my perspective with you when you ask. Trust me, child. I will fulfill your hopes more sweetly than you can imagine. Don't look away from my loving-kindness for a moment, and you will never need to worry. There is no risk of failure in me because I never falter. You have tasted of my goodness, but you are not finished yet. There is always more for you. Press into my heart today and feast on my affection!

Keep trusting in the Lord and do what is right in his eyes.
Fix your heart on the promises of God and you will be secure,
feasting on his faithfulness.

PSALM 37:3

My glory transforms you.

A s you feast on my glorious presence within you, you cannot help but transform into my likeness. In my light, you become light. Bring everything to me today. Bring me your attitude, your desires, your disappointments, your joys. Bring them all and watch as I illuminate each one in the radiance of my love-light. If you are empty, come and be filled. If you are full, you are welcome to the overflow.

Nothing in your life is exempt from my marvelous mercy. Not a crack will remain unfilled. Fellowship with me in this very moment and find the strength and satisfaction you've been awaiting. It's never too soon, and it's never too late to come into my presence. If you come in weeping, I will lead you out in peace. If you come in with thanksgiving, I will fill you with joy. I withhold no good thing from my beloved ones. If you will only let your eyes open to see the fruit of my kindness within and all around you, you will see that I never stop pouring my goodness over you.

Be transformed as you embrace the glorious Christ-within as your new life and live in union with him! For God has recreated you all over again in his perfect righteousness.

EPHESIANS 4:24

AUGUST 15

My presence always satisfies.

Beloved, I have given you the fullness of my presence—my Spirit alive within you. Today tune into the peace of my goodness that is already at work in you. Turn your attention to me, and direct the path of your thoughts toward my abundant love. As you look to me, the well of living water inside of you will flood the landscape of your heart, refreshing the dry and worn-out places.

There's no need to go searching throughout the earth for satisfaction that lasts. I am your plentiful portion, your abundant hope and true peace. Open wide the gates of your heart to my glory-light, and the purity of my presence will refresh you. I never hide my face from those who seek to know me in spirit and in truth. Let me satisfy you with the wisdom of my Word that feeds your pursuit of my kingdom ways. Come alive in the light of my love. I am nearer than your breath and closer than your skin. You are saturated in my mercy, child. Rejoice in this precious communion!

Out of your innermost being is flowing the fullness of my Spirit—
never failing to satisfy.

Song of Songs 7:2

Hope holds you.

The garment of my grace wraps around you today. My goodness is the floor beneath your feet, my favor like a wraparound shield. You are living in the light of my mercy, so let its radiance soak your soul with confident peace. Whether your heart is overwhelmed with sorrow or is full of joy, I meet you in every state you're in. I am your refuge of reliable strength. Even when you are struggling to hold onto hope, hope holds onto you!

You cannot escape the support of my love—even if you were to try, you would not get beyond its reach. I hold you together when you feel like you might fall apart. I restore, redeem, and resurrect retired dreams into orchards of fantastic fruit. Nothing in your life remains untouched by my miracle-working power. Submit your heart to me once again and find the refreshment of my perspective in place of your own. Put all your confidence in me. I am at work in the details of your life, and I am lacing it all together with the thread of my glorious loving-kindness.

He's the hope that holds me and the Stronghold to shelter me,
the only God for me, and my great confidence.

PSALM 91:2

My plans will surprise you.

When your life is bound to mine in surrender, you will find that I lead you along paths of living understanding. My wisdom will light each step you take. Even so, you will not know every twist and turn that is ahead. But I see it all. Even when you walk through the wilderness, I am with you. When the fog of loss descends, I will carry you through. Though weeping may last for a night-season, joy will come in the dawning of a new day.

There is goodness sown into the fabric of your life—can you see it? It is but a foretaste of what is to come. You never need to worry about provision, for you will have all that you need. I take care of my loyal lovers. I see the scope of your life, and I know how to guide you along the pathway of my loving-kindness every step of the way. The dreams you have for your life will pale in comparison to the glorious reality of what awaits you—both here and into eternity!

I am Wisdom, and I am shrewd and intelligent.
I have at my disposal living-understanding
to devise a plan for your life.
PROVERBS 8:12

Choose me over your comfort.

As the One who called you to this surrendered life, I am trustworthy to guide you through it. As you lean on me and my understanding, I will empower you to walk in the way of love with every step. Submit your ways to mine, and you will find that your life is overflowing with mercy and grace. I have called you to an overcoming life, but you cannot overcome the world by your own strength. You must rely on my power at work within you to do it, and you have access to my limitless might through fellowship with my Spirit.

You have heard it said that my ways are above your human ways and my thoughts are higher than your own. This is true. I know you better than you know yourself, and I will lead you into everlasting life as you depend on me. Greater joy is yours through my Spirit-life than any you could imagine experiencing outside of me. There is fulfillment of every longing. No one can escape pain in this life, but you can also experience endless delight in me as you venture through it. So join your life to mine in full surrender today.

If you truly want to follow me, you should at once completely reject and disown your own life. And you must be willing to share my cross and experience it as your own, as you continually surrender to my ways.

MATTHEW 16:24

My love keeps you tender.

Come to me, and I will give you rest. I surround you with my wraparound presence and pull you in with tender love. As I continually refresh you in my mercy, you will find it so much easier to offer compassion to others. Let my love fill you up to overflow, and you will always have more than enough kindness to show.

As you live in the abundance of my compassionate heart, it will be impossible for you to keep it all to yourself. Look through the lens of my love. Search out my wisdom, for it is right at hand. Though this world does not celebrate mercy in the same way it celebrates grit and drive, know that compassion will last forever. The return of your sacrificial love will be sweeter than any accolades you could get from achieving status or success by the world's standards. Let my love continue to change you, and you will change the world with kindness, even if it is just your corner of it. Be generous, beloved, as I am generous.

Show mercy and compassion for others, just as your heavenly
Father overflows with mercy and compassion for all.

LUKE 6:36

Let me move your heart.

D aughter, you are my beloved one. I long to show you my love in a new way today, so let me increase your understanding of the depths of my kindness. There is no one else in all the earth like you. I created you in my image, so you bear my likeness. Your heart that holds compassion for others is reflective of my own. The way your laughter lights up a room speaks of my joy in you. You have an intricate mind that sees details that others miss. Your beauty is more than skin-deep; it radiates from within.

I could spend a thousand years pouring my love over you, and it would be like a drop in the bucket. My love does not require anything from you, but it will change you. My mercy has marked you, beloved. Let your heart open up like a blooming flower in the light of my affectionate gaze. Turn to me, and you will never be disappointed by what you are met with. If you let me, I will love you to life over and over again.

May the Lord move your hearts into a greater understanding
of God's pure love for you and into Christ's steadfast endurance.

2 THESSALONIANS 3:5

Find yourself in me.

Daughter, do not lose yourself in another. When you look for someone else to fill pieces of you, you will find that you lose sight of what you already have. I have made you whole. You are complete in my love. No other love can fill you up, feed your identity, and set you free all at the same time.

Though you are limited in love, I am not. I created you to be fully alive in the goodness of my heart. There is no place you could run where my kindness has not already gone. Lesser loves will never satisfy the way I do. I will not hurt or manipulate you. I never change my mind about choosing you. You are mine—for now and for always. Let your heart find its freedom in the ocean of my joy and delight. I will never turn you away. There will never be a moment in this day when I do not welcome you in with open arms. Come alive in my love, beloved one, and be free!

Our own completeness is now found in him. We are completely filled with God as Christ's fullness overflows within us. He is the Head of every kingdom and authority in the universe!

COLOSSIANS 2:10

Rejoice in your forgiveness.

Y ou are my own, brought into oneness with me through the blood of Jesus. Nothing could have kept you from my lavish love, for it has been pursuing you since you were formed in your mother's womb. No power on earth or anywhere else can keep you from living in the purity of your purpose. All chains of sin and death were broken when Christ raised up in resurrection power. You are free in mercy, my child. You are alive in me, so rejoice in your freedom!

My power has left no sin-cycle untouched. Love has liberated you. So where there are echoes of captivity, surrender to my powerful mercy. Watch! I will wash away the remnants of shame as you walk in the light of my life. Align your life with mine, letting go of everything that would hinder love's call, and run in the radiance of my glory. With uninterrupted connection, live with your heart open to my voice and to my leading. I will never let you go or let you down. Even if you find yourself on an old, worn-out path that leads to darkness, I will guide you back to liberty again.

We were held in sin's grasp. But now, we've been resurrected out of that "realm of death" never to return, for we are forever alive and forgiven of all our sins!

Colossians 2:13

I give peace that lasts.

C ome close, child, and remind your heart of my lasting truth. Drink deeply of my delight as I speak my words of life over you. I do not give like the world gives—temporary fixes for finite periods. When I offer you something, it is better than any other could give. My loving nature knows no limits; my mercy has no end. You could spend your entire life trying to exhaust my patience, but you would never be able to talk me out of my compassion.

Nothing comes between our fellowship. Nothing can interrupt our communion. Nothing can separate you from my loyal love. For Christ has ushered you into relationship with me, and you cannot outrun my faithfulness. Here I offer you peace of mind and heart that rests on my unfailing nature—not on yours. Take hope today as you receive a fresh portion of my wisdom. When you eat of my revelation-knowledge, you will also taste the confidence of my everlasting peace.

Our faith in Jesus transfers God's righteousness to us and he now declares us flawless in his eyes. This means we can now enjoy true and lasting peace with God.

ROMANS 5:1

Come as you are.

B eloved, come as you are to my table. There is no need to dress yourself up or tone yourself down. Just as you are is how I will receive you every time. Drink from the cup in my hand. You have access to my never-ending kindness whenever you need it. I offer you the closeness of relationship that Spirit, Son, and Father have. What is mine is yours.

You will find true belonging here in my fellowship. You are fully known, wholly accepted, and completely loved by me, your Creator and your friend. Let down all of your defenses. There is no need to explain a thing to me, for I know you, inside and out. Don't let fear keep you from accepting my untainted affection. Let down the walls and let me in. Even now, do you see that you already have my favor? There's nothing to earn here. It's all yours already. I promise that I am a tender and wise Counselor. Feast on my rich love that I lay out in plenty before you. There's no need to wait on my cue. Just eat up whenever you like.

I give you your destiny: I am promising you the kingdom realm that the Father has promised me. We will celebrate in this kingdom and you will feast with me at my table.

Luke 22:29–30

I never lead you into temptation.

C hild, do not let discouragement deceive you. When you are tempted, it is not my doing. In fact, it is I who leads you out of it. I always provide my loyal lovers with a way to stand up under every single temptation that comes their way. I am the God of all wisdom and insight, and I will give you eyes to see the kindness of my constant help. Look to me!

I am known for my mercy throughout the ages, and I will never change. Count on me to bring you through every trial and hardship. I will never abandon you in the midst of your mess. Cling to me, for I am always close. I have not left you, beloved. Let your heart find rest and confidence in my faithful love. Be encouraged and full of hope today, for you have not reached the end of my goodness. Consider my kindness and my merciful nature. I am with you, leading you into deliverance and freedom from fear. Stand tall in the light of my love.

When you are tempted don't ever say, "God is tempting me,"
for God is incapable of being tempted by evil
and he is never the source of temptation.

JAMES 1:13

Be true in love.

Drink in the deep delight of my heart today. Fill up on my unending kindness. Feast on my compassion. Does it feel like I'm pushing you too hard to receive? It is only because the more you receive, the more you have to give. I don't want the well of your heart to run dry because you feel as if you have to stir up love on your own. First drink from my living waters, and you will find that you have more than enough to offer others.

When you find yourself laboring to love those around you, it is a sign that you need to turn your heart toward me in surrender. Let me water the garden of your heart with the showers of my mercy. There's no need to strive to love. Your choices matter—of course they do. But you have the resource of unending love at hand. Let your soul come alive in the light of my kindness, and you will find that kindness flows freely from you. There's no need to pretend. Just be true in love by allowing me to refill you constantly. Keep coming back to me and drinking up every chance you get.

Let the inner movement of your heart always be to love one another, and never play the role of an actor wearing a mask. Despise evil and embrace everything that is good and virtuous.

ROMANS 12:9

Continue walking in my ways.

Continue to walk along the path I have laid out for you. It is full of my goodness. Though others may criticize your choices, do not give up following my higher ways. Few choose to walk the way of laid-down love, for the path is narrow. Even if you are the only one in your world choosing to follow me, I promise it will be worth it in the end. I keep track of every surrender and every movement of mercy in your life. Soon you will see that the fruit of your submission to love is sweet and the rewards are lasting.

When you walk in purity of purpose, you will find the demands are not too great. And whenever you find yourself out of your depth, you have my resources to fill, strengthen, and support you. Keep me as your vision, your eyes fixed on my loyal love. Though others may achieve short-term success in their own right, it is not a satisfaction that lasts. Set your hopes on me, for I will satisfy the desires of your heart. Follow along my pathway of peace, and you will have joy as your constant companion. You will have nothing to worry about, for your God is the well you drink from and your guard forever.

Even if the princes and my leaders choose to criticize me,
I will continue to serve you and walk in your plans for my life.
PSALM 119:23

You are whole.

C hild, you are wholly and fully found in me. You do not consist of a bunch of broken pieces, held flimsily together by the glue of wishful thinking. My mercy has filled in every crack with the liquid gold of my presence. You are whole, and you are beautiful to behold. Your life is a reflection of my redemption power at work.

Bring me every part of you that feels out of sync, and I will align it in my perfect love. There is nothing that won't come alive when I breathe my Spirit's life into it. Give me your broken dreams, your shattered hopes, and every discouragement of your soul. Bring me your joys, your comforts, and your gratitude as well. It is all a part of your story, and I am weaving it together with the thread of my mercy. I am resurrecting your hope as I breathe my persistent promise into your spirit. You are mine, you are beloved, and you are whole. I will always refresh you and continually renew you with the oil of my love. No, you are not broken, daughter. Not even a little.

My child, if you truly want a long and satisfying life,
never forget the things that I've taught you.
Follow closely every truth that I've given you.
Then you will have a full, rewarding life.

PROVERBS 3:1–2

You belong to the light.

Beloved, you are a child of the kingdom of light. You belong to the source of life itself. Let the radiance of my glory flood your life with pure hope and clear vision. You do not belong to any other. Do not let the shadows overtake you, for you are already alive in love's light. Rise up in your freedom, beloved. Let your heart take confidence in your identity as daughter of God. You are a pure reflection of my kindness.

Today let your heart come alive with hope. Let joy fill your soul to overflowing, for you are the delight of my heart. Lay down everything that hinders love in your life, and I will give you gifts of goodness. What is mine is yours. You have not been brought into a kingdom to serve the whims of a careless king. You are a part of my family, and I care deeply for everything that moves your own heart. You will find your desires fulfilled in me, for I don't miss a thing. Rise up and shine, daughter, for you are a living light!

You are all children of the light and children of the day.
We don't belong to the night nor to darkness.

1 THESSALONIANS 5:5

Train in righteousness.

When you walk in the ways of my kingdom, you represent a living light among the shadows of this world. It is good to devote energy toward growing in goodness by spending time in fellowship with my Spirit and by ingesting my living Word. You cannot go wrong when you spend time training in the methods of my love and mercy. Let your focus narrow as you hone in on my wisdom.

Have you already experienced some of the benefits of growing closer to me? I have so much more to offer. As you train, you will grow stronger in faith. As you practice continual surrender, my great grace will empower you for every situation you face. This is the place where you learn to lean on my power. Then when testing comes, you will already have the muscle memory of relying on me. You lack nothing to live a godly life, modeled after the totally surrendered love of Christ. The power that raised him from the grave lives inside of you. Find your focus here in my presence and be filled up!

Athletic training only benefits you for a short season,
but righteousness brings lasting benefit in everything;
for righteousness contains the promise of life,
for time and eternity.

1 TIMOTHY 4:8

Wait for me to move.

Take courage today in my faithfulness as you wait on me to break through for you. I never abandon my beloved ones, and I certainly do not leave you to fight for yourself. Stir up hope, for I am calling you to rest in me as I act on your behalf. Do you remember my faithfulness in days gone by? I am the same. No, I have not changed. I am in the details of your life, even the places that you cannot see. I am the restorer, and I am touching every needy area with my mercy. You will rejoice when you see what I have done!

Let your heart become more and more confident in my goodness as you trust my perfect ways and timing. I am your ever-present help in times of trouble. I am never early or too late—only right on time. Trust me, even in the mystery. Lean on my understanding even when you can't grasp its scope. I see all things with clarity, and my mercy motivates everything I do. Do not despair or lose hope, for I am working all things out for your good and benefit. I promise I will never sway from my purposes for your life.

Lord, the only thing I can do is wait and put my hope in you.
I wait for your help, my God.

PSALM 38:15

September

Compassion is your calling.

When you look through the eyes of my love into the situations and people in your life, you are invited into the compassion of my heart. There is no greater calling than the call to love. When you feel inclined to judge, turn to me, and I will offer you the lens of my lavish affection that melts even the coldest heart. Walk in the way of love in every relationship, and you will find my goodness there.

When those around you are struggling to believe, do not force faith upon them. Instead, offer them the same kindness I offer you. Faithful fellowship flourishes in companionship and wisdom. Lean into my love, and you will have more than enough to offer others. You don't need to have all the answers in order to love people well. It is time to put away the pressure of perfectionism, which I have never required. Mercy and wisdom always work together, and I will teach you to walk hand in hand with them. Above all, fill this day with conscious compassion that reaches out instead of furious fear that withdraws from others. Let love be the force that compels you; it will increase your understanding of my heart.

Keep being compassionate
to those who still have doubts.

JUDE 22

Let my love overwhelm you.

Beloved, stand under the waterfall of my mercy today and let it wash away all the dust of the world that has settled on you. As my peace pours over you, every worry loses its weight. As the flow of my lavish love catches you, every fear faints away. There is no hurry in this place. Let the calming pool of my faithfulness catch every stray thought. You are my own—my pleasure and my delight. I never leave you alone, striving to work things out in your own strength. The life you long for is already accessible in the free fellowship you have with my Spirit.

As my love purifies you, can't you see that my ways for you are simple? My mercy love offering is an open channel of strength for you at all times. Lay down the need to do things perfectly. Why would you require perfection when I don't? Don't pick things back up that you once freely gave to me. Do not let shame take hold of you, for you have been set free in my love. My correction comes with kindness. I have lifted you up, so don't beat yourself down. Walk in the ways of my peace, with others, with me, and with yourself. Join your life to mine at all times, and you will never need to struggle on your own again.

May God's mercy, peace, and love
cascade over you!

JUDE 2

I am easy to please.

Beloved, walk in the way of love. Pursue peace and look to me in whatever you do. You will find that all the details work themselves out as you follow on my pathway of peace. I am easy to please. I don't make my nature a mystery or require you to follow a long list of rules. Simply allow yourself to be infused with the strength of my Spirit living inside of you. Let my grace empower you to follow through in compassion and to extend mercy to any who require it. Don't forget that you are included in this.

I will always lead you in love, so stay teachable as I gently correct you along the way. Let your heart be humble just as I am humble. Find joy in simple things; rejoice with the ones you love. When you know who I am, it is easy for you to become like me. Don't worry, for I will help you whenever you need it. I won't grow tired of your missteps or questions. Stay in close fellowship with me, and you will never need to wonder about the state you're in.

Simply join your life with mine.
Learn my ways and you'll discover
that I'm gentle, humble, easy to please.
You will find refreshment and rest in me.

MATTHEW 11:29

Surrender and find true freedom.

I n the light of my life, you find true freedom. The ways of my kingdom are full of wisdom and clarity. The ways of this world will lead you to empty promises and unfulfilled hopes. Nothing will satisfy the heart that always reaches for the next thing instead of delighting in what it already has. If never-enough is the tune of your motivation, then, my child, it is time to recalibrate in my love.

Surrender to my kingdom ways, and you will find life's meaning in my delight. Every question you have will find its answer in my limitless mercy. You cannot escape the power of my transformative love when I call you my own. So align your life with mine, and even when you can't clearly understand my purposes, you will live in the fruit of my gracious heart. You see in part and know in part, but I see everything clearly. I am pure in wisdom and motive, and my mercy informs all that I do. You will find all your desires fulfilled in me—even ones you don't know are driving your life. Trust me; I know you better than you know yourself.

The person who loves his life and pampers himself will miss true life! But the one who detaches his life from this world and abandons himself to me, will find true life and enjoy it forever!

JOHN 12:25

Weakness is not failure.

As long as you walk the dirt of this earth, you will find that your abilities will waver in different seasons. But, beloved, don't feel discouraged when your frailty brings you to your knees. I am your constant and steady support. A river of grace flows from my throne, and you are caught up in its tide. Look through my lens of love and you will see that every time you are depleted of your own will to go on, I empower you with my strength.

Do not despise your weakness, beloved. Remember I am a good Father. What parent would watch his child struggle and not offer support and solutions? Even if one would, that is not how I operate. You have my Spirit with you at all times. My living love is active within you. I pour out fresh mercies every morning. Each moment is a new opportunity to lean on my strong love. Know that I am with you, I am for you, and I am the source of all that you need. Stop trying to do it all on your own and instead partner with me. I do all the heavy lifting.

> He answered me, "My grace is always more than enough for you, and my power finds its full expression through your weakness."… When I'm weak I sense more deeply the mighty power of Christ living in me.
>
> 2 CORINTHIANS 12:9

Let me be your confidence.

I am your good and faithful Father. I will never let you slip from my grip of grace or let your life go down a dark road where my light cannot reach. You are forever found in my mercy. My limitless love surrounds you. Instead of your own abilities, let my faithfulness be your confidence. I will never fail you; no, I will never neglect my Word.

Some trust in the strength of their intellect or the power of their alliances. You are a child of the King of kings. All power is subject to the weakness of its source, but I have no weaknesses. Where others inevitably fall, I never do. My Word stands firm forever, and nothing can thwart my purposes. My mercy covers every vulnerability you have, so there's no need to fear what will come when you build your hopes on the firm foundation of my unfailing love. Do not hesitate to run to me with whatever troubles you face. I will not turn you away or refuse to help. I am your ever-present support. Lean on me, and you will not fall.

We have boldness through him, and free access as kings before the Father because of our complete confidence in Christ's faithfulness.

EPHESIANS 3:12

I keep watch over you.

Draw near to the peace of my presence, where I bring into clear view everything that is out of focus. What is the hesitation in your heart today? Fear will keep you on edge, feeling like the ball will drop at any moment. Though you have been conditioned to keep watch, you can hand that responsibility over to me. I will not let chaos ambush you.

When you find your security in me, nothing can shake it. I will keep you safe, beloved. You can trust me. Are you holding on to the unknowns? Do you believe that you can control them if you keep them always before your eyes? Let them go. I say it again—you can trust me. Follow my gentle leadership. Storms will not break you, for I am your shelter. Wars will not decimate your spirit, for I am your Defender and your perfect peace. I will bring the chaos of this world to rest and lead you into my glorious kingdom of light and everlasting life. Let me be the watch keeper of your heart as you cultivate what is growing there in the rich soil of my love. Spend time now digging in the garden of delight where you will find the fruit of my faithfulness.

He will keep you from every form of evil or calamity
as he continually watches over you.

PSALM 121:7

My power changes everything.

I am the power of life itself, the source of all that was, is, and is to come. I am not limited to the laws of this nature, for I wrote them in the first place. I am the giver of good things, and the One who restores all things to glory. I make all things new because it's what I do. I am Creator. Even so, the power that is at work in holding the stars in their places is the same power at work in your life. I am making you new, reviving your courage, and restoring your identity as child of the living God.

When I speak, who can contest it? When I move, who can stop me? I am doing a new thing in your life, bringing victory and loveliness out of the ashes of defeat. I am redeeming every broken dream in my lavish love. Come alive in the sweetness of my delight. There is no shadow of a doubt in my mind about choosing you as my own. You are my beloved, my child, my chosen. The power of my life within you breaks down the cycles of trauma and shame. Your destiny is greater than you know. You are free to be who I created you to be—free in me.

I continually long to know the wonders of Jesus more fully and to experience the overflowing power of his resurrection working in me.

PHILIPPIANS 3:10

Cling to me.

D o not give up the surrendering of your heart to my wide-open gates of endless grace. There is no shortage of supply in my storehouse of plenty. When the winds of adversity blow, turn your face toward me, and I will tuck you under my arm, covering you in the garment of my mercy. The winds will never blow you away when you are this close. I have got you.

Cling to me with all you have. No matter what, I have a tight grip on your life. When you grab hold with your own hands, you will feel the weight of my nearness, building confidence in your heart. Keep your soul close to my heart, and you will always have everything you need. Press in, feel the beat of my heart against your cheek. It is steady and strong, not racing or fearful. Let your heart sync to the rhythm of my own as you rest in my constant care. You are safe here. You will always be securely found in my protective embrace.

> With passion I pursue and cling to you.
> Because I feel your grip on my life,
> I keep my soul close to your heart.
>
> PSALM 63:8

Let my wisdom guide you.

L et the good fruit of a surrendered heart fill your life to the brim. You walk in the ways of my wisdom when you model your life after my nature. Be quick in mercy, offering forgiveness to those who wrong you. Look for cords of compassion that bind you to others in love. Be kind to all, not basing your attitude on what someone may offer you. Fill up on my loyal love, and you will always have more than enough to give away.

Be generous in sympathy as I am generous in compassionate comfort whenever you need it. Bring all your burdens to me on a daily basis—over and over again. I will lift the weight of offenses and frustrations and give you eyes to see with my perfect perspective. Build up your faith through fellowship with other laid-down lovers. Let my power flow through your life in open connection with my Spirit. You have everything you need for a good and godly life already. Focus in on me, and you will not waver from my pathway of peace.

If you consider yourself to be wise and one who understands the ways of God, advertise it with a beautiful, fruitful life guided by wisdom's gentleness.

JAMES 3:13

My goodness restores you.

Come to my refreshing waters and drink deeply of my love today. I will restore you in loving-kindness and flood your mind with the peace of my presence. I am abundant life, and you have unrestricted access to me through Jesus. You have been made new in my mercy-stream.

Whenever you are weary, come and rest in my loyal love. You will find your soul revived every time. I lead you into my gardens of grace where you can feast on the fruit of my Spirit. It is sweet to the taste and full of nutrients to build your faith. Don't hold back from my presence that awakens your soul to life. Turn your attention to me, and you will see that I am always attentive toward you. You are my beloved, and my mercy is not finished with you yet. Come alive in my delight and walk in the wonder of my ways. My faithfulness will lead you into the overwhelming joy of my kingdom come.

That's where he restores and revives my life. He opens before me pathways to God's pleasure and leads me along in his footsteps of righteousness so that I can bring honor to his name.

PSALM 23:3

SEPTEMBER 12

I am so very near.

Beloved, I am the God who draws close to you in every season of the soul. I am near to the brokenhearted and so very close to those who are suffering. I am with you in your overwhelming joy and in your present pain. I wrap around you with the comfort of my love that covers you with kindness. You are tucked into the blanket of my mercy. No force can separate you from my affection. You are called *chosen*; you are mine. I will never leave you. I never disown my children.

Lean on my strength. Yes, I will support you. I never force my kindness upon you, though it covers you all the same. Let your heart take hope in my presence. Let your faith arise in the landscape of my loyal love. Look for the gemstones of my goodness hidden within your life. Build up gratitude, stone by stone. It will change your perspective even as I hold you close. I am your strong and mighty Defender, so rest in my victory over your life.

God, our hearts spill over with praise to you!
We overflow with thanks, for your name is the "Near One."

PSALM 75:1

I am acting on your behalf.

There is no need to give in to worry today. Come close and be comforted by my wraparound presence. I surround you with loving-kindness, hemming you in behind and before. Lay down your built-up defenses at my feet. Let me be the One to defend you. Rest in my peace as I work out every tough situation to grow you in love and benefit you in the end.

Wrap my grace around your heart and refuse to get even on your own. Resist the urge to stir the chaos, adding to its effects in your life. Choose mercy instead of vengeance. Choose all-giving-love instead of protecting your pride. I am more than able to turn every situation around with my powerful redemption and defense of your identity. Don't give in to despair when it seems like others are getting away with the harmful tactics they wield. For their day is coming, and I am the One they will face. Let me work it out. You can rest in the confidence of my faithfulness.

Don't ever say, "I'm going to get even with them
if it's the last thing I do!"
Wrap God's grace around your heart
and he will be the one to vindicate you.
PROVERBS 20:22

Follow my footsteps.

Follow me into the sanctuary of my presence. I am not far. Whenever you don't know what to do, follow the path already laid out for you. You are acquainted with wisdom, and she will never lead you astray. The path of love always leads to me; compassion and mercy meet in my presence. You cannot go wrong when you choose to imitate the kindness in my nature.

You know by now that my burden is light, and I take every heavy load that you pick up along the way. Come to the place of rest, the refuge of my love. What is required of you is not complicated, for it is as simple as following me. Though my love is a mystery, my ways are not. They are clear, though to those who do not know me, they may seem foolish. Extend mercy to those whom the world ignores, and you will find that I am already there at work in their hearts. Model your life after mine, and you will always be found in the flood of my favor.

Listen, my radiant one—
if you ever lose sight of me,
just follow in my footsteps where I lead my lovers.
Come with your burdens and cares.
Come to the place near the sanctuary of my shepherds.

SONG OF SONGS 1:8

Live out your faith.

As I speak my words of promise over your life, how you respond dictates the development of your faith, though it cannot change my faithfulness. Grow in your understanding by imitating what you have already learned. Let my love fuel yours as you live out my kingdom principles. My kindness shields you. Even if you were to fail in all of your endeavors, mercy would have you covered. Walk in the way of love, and you will not stumble.

Remember, daughter, that perfection is never the goal. You learn by doing. So practice what you have stored up in your heart by feasting on my goodness. You have been soaking in wisdom's light, now let it shine through your life. Endless grace is available to you, but grace isn't of much use to someone who believes she can make it on her own. Now is the time to step out and build your faith by living what you have been learning. Be free in my love!

Don't just listen to the Word of Truth and not respond to it, for that is the essence of self-deception. So always let his Word become like poetry written and fulfilled by your life!

JAMES 1:22

Hold onto hope.

Beloved, I am not known as the faithful One for nothing. Trust me and align your heart in hope with my promises. Though the waiting seems long, I am at work in the details. I will not withhold my goodness from you even when you waver and begin to wonder if my timing is indeed perfect. Your questions do not offend me. I never act in spite toward my beloved ones. You cannot complain your way out of my faithfulness, though you can talk yourself out of peace in the waiting.

It is coming, when the daybreak of your promise dawns and you are living in your dream come true. You will be living in the joy of hopes fulfilled. Until that day, don't let go of the hope that keeps your heart reaching toward me. You can trust that my promises never fail. I love you so much more than you could imagine, and I give better than good gifts to each one of my children. Let the expectation of your heart match my faithfulness, and you will rejoice now, even in the waiting.

When hope's dream seems to drag on and on,
the delay can be depressing.
But when at last your dream comes true,
life's sweetness will satisfy your soul.

PROVERBS 13:12

I give you heavenly insight.

Are you looking for insight? Are you hungry for wisdom? Open up your heart and let my revelation-light shine on you. My living Word will sharpen your perspective and give you eyes to see into my ways. Integrity will be the lining of your life as you apply my kingdom principles to how you live out my love.

You need never dwell on the shame of your past sins when you align your life with mine. Though the world may not understand your choices, you remain in the steadfast flow of my mercy-tide. Do you have questions? Ask away. Do you have concerns? Lay them out before me. When you seek my higher perspective, I will give you the keys of wisdom to unlock solutions for the problems you face. I am full of insight to all who eagerly look for it. Feast on the fellowship of divine connection within you. I am speaking even now. If ever you doubt my voice, look into my Word, and you will find clarity for your understanding. There is so much life for you here in the communion of your spirit and mine. Behold, I am Light, and I make all things clear.

Break open your word within me until revelation-light shines out!
Those with open hearts are given insight into your plans.

PSALM 119:130

My glory outweighs every trial.

Look and see what I am doing for all of my loyal lovers. Seek out the testimonies of my beloved ones, and you will find that I am at work in the chaos and faithfully moving in the midst of every crisis. Fix your eyes on the eternal—that which lasts. You already know that the shifting winds of seasons cause tides and moods to rise and fall. What is here today may be gone tomorrow. Why put all your hope in things you can see when they will eventually fade?

No, my child, let your confidence be found in that which will never rust or be destroyed. You have been born into an eternal kingdom full of light and life. My glory shines brighter than the sun on all of my beloved ones. Do not despair when you walk through times of testing, for I am your good and present help at all times. Let your joy be in the lasting fruit of my Spirit. Store up for yourself treasures that will never fade as you lay down your life in loyal love. My path leads to fullness, so keep pressing on!

We don't focus our attention on what is seen but on what is unseen. For what is seen is temporary, but the unseen realm is eternal.

2 CORINTHIANS 4:18

Worship your way to strength.

W hen you run out of options and you don't know what else to do, praise your way to peace. When you worship with childlike faith, you open up a highway to my presence. Praise pulls down my promises as you fix your heart and mind on my everlasting goodness. Let your mouth sing the simple praises that overflow from the hearts of my loyal lovers. You will find your faith strengthened as you sing about my faithfulness. As you meditate with song on the marvelous mercy of my nature, you break the stronghold of fear and shame. The sound of your freedom song releases my power.

Let the words of your mouth reflect the surrender of your heart to my unfailing love. My kindness covers you. When you line up your life with my wonderful ways, the projection of your faith is even more powerful. Sing along with creation in thanksgiving, and offer your highest praise. You will find your soul strengthened and the arrows of doubt caught in the shield of faith as you offer your living sacrifice of worship.

Strength rises up with the chorus of singing children. This kind of praise has the power to shut Satan's mouth. Childlike worship will silence the madness of those who oppose you.

PSALM 8:2

Let prayer change you.

Beloved, let the saturation of my love soften your heart. As you devote yourself to fellowship with me through prayer, you will find that the oil of my mercy purifies your desires. You cannot constantly commune with me and remain unchanged. So whatever you do, do it with an open heart of surrender that looks to my wisdom for guidance.

There's no need to censor yourself with me, for I already know the deepest part of your heart anyway. Nothing you could say would surprise me. You have access to all of me. If you give my Spirit the same access, my life inside of you will change you. Cultivate the growth of the fruit of my Spirit as you soak in the radiance of my presence. Let gratitude and kindness be the words that coax your own growth, and always be gentle with yourself as I am with you. And in all things, welcome me in. The garden of your heart thrives in the communion of deep calling to deep, Spirit to spirit.

Don't be pulled in different directions or worried about a thing.
Be saturated in prayer throughout each day, offering your faith-filled
requests before God with overflowing gratitude.

PHILIPPIANS 4:6

My Word is a sharp sword.

A s you use the Word as your weapon, you learn to wield the power of my Spirit. There is no need to rely on your own abilities and strengths when you have mine within reach. When you don't know what to do, dig into the wisdom of my Word. Remind yourself of my promises by writing them on the tablet of your heart. Keep them at hand where you can easily stir them up, for they are living and active.

As you ingest the insights I give, you will grow in confidence to wage war against the temporal temptations you face. The sword of my Spirit cuts down every lie of the enemy. It is sharp enough to separate flesh from bone; it is a powerful tool in the hands of my beloved ones. Keep my living Word stirring in your heart and at the forefront of your thoughts. It is the best weapon you have to take down the inventions of the enemy in every situation. Be ready to speak my truth at all times because it will save you from needless arguments and dead-end doubts. And keep praying, for it sharpens your sword-wielding skills.

Take the mighty razor-sharp Spirit-sword
of the spoken Word of God.
Pray passionately in the Spirit,
as you constantly intercede
with every form of prayer at all times.
EPHESIANS 6:17–18

Write down your revelation.

K eep a record of the insights I reveal to you through my living Word. They will stir your heart when you look them over later and remember the simplicity of my wisdom at work in your life. When I speak and you feel the profound weight behind the meaning of my words, that is revelation-knowledge. That is the light of my glory giving you understanding.

Build yourself up in faith by documenting your prayers and my answers. It is not for my benefit but for yours. Your confidence grows in the soil of my faithfulness. Why not keep a map of my goodness in your life to help yourself connect to your conviction all the more? Though you see in part, you will trust more readily when you are reminded. Let your heart be encouraged as you recall all that I have spoken and, even more, all that I have done. You are my beloved, and I love to fulfill my promises to you. I always answer your cries for help.

I consider your prophecies to be my greatest treasure,
and I memorize them and write them on my heart
to keep me from committing sin's treason against you.

PSALM 119:11

Join my ministry of reconciliation.

I am the God of the turnaround. I redeem that which seems utterly lost and restore it to connection with me, the source of its birth. I am the God who throws into the sea of forgetfulness every record of wrong held against my beloved ones. I do not keep count of transgressions; wrongdoing does not inform my mercy. My mercy-flow is a tidal wave that overtakes all in its path, though instead of bringing destruction, it brings life.

Join with me in my mission to reconcile all who have waded in the ocean of waywardness back into right relationship with me. All you have to do is point the way for them whenever you have the opportunity. I have already done the work of restoration. Just as Jesus instructed those he taught to follow after him, you have also followed along the pathway of laid-down love. You know the way to peace with me, so join with my heart in reaching out to those who have not yet understood my great kindness. Point others to the path in love, and you will be walking in the confident compassion of my mercy. Partner with me, as I have already partnered with you.

It was through the Anointed One that God was shepherding the world, not even keeping records of their transgressions, and he has entrusted to us the ministry of opening the door of reconciliation to God.

2 CORINTHIANS 5:19

Compare your troubles to me.

My character is full of loving-kindness, constant and true. My mercy knows no boundaries; there is no beginning or end to it. I am the embodiment of love itself. My power holds the universe together even as it keeps expanding. There is nothing created that I did not first speak into existence. You were a thought in my mind before you became flesh and blood. Yet here you are, in fellowship with your maker and God.

When you consider the majesty of my marvelous wonders and the glory of my powerful ways, what trouble could stand against me? What could compare to my infinite and strong love? Think about this, your momentary trials are but a fleeting memory when time has passed. Why would you let worry weigh you down when I am on your side? I am with you, and I will never leave you. Remember who I am and what I am capable of. What concern could hold off your confident expectation in me? Trust me and let go of anxiety today. I have got you.

The Son is the dazzling radiance of God's splendor, the exact expression of God's true nature—his mirror image! He holds the universe together and expands it by the mighty power of his spoken word.

HEBREWS 1:3

Your character is being forged.

Y ou follow closely in my footsteps when you choose to persevere in the path of faith. I will never lead you somewhere I have not already gone myself. I am your good guide. I am always by your side, supporting you whenever you need it. Lean on me, especially in the days when your patience is being tested. As you practice endurance, the fire of my love refines you. You are purified in purpose, and your perspective is aligned in my great mercy where there is abundant room to mature in me.

The wilderness of waiting shapes your character. Don't resist the testing, but rather invite my powerful presence into your process. You have everything you need in me to grow in love, hope, and grace. My Spirit thrives on the wonders of breakthrough, so there will be no lack of miracles from my powerful life inside of you. What areas look impossibly defeated right now? Which places of your life are without hope apart from me? Those are the places of your breakthrough and of my miracle deliverance. In the waiting, press into me, and I will deliver you. I will do what only I can do as you persistently hope in my unfailing love. Hold on because everything has a purpose in my plan of redemption.

Patient endurance will refine our character,
and proven character leads us back to hope.

ROMANS 5:4

Listen to me.

Beloved, come to me today and spend time soaking in my presence. I am full of wisdom for every situation you face. I give living-understanding to those who seek me, so sit at my feet in the secret place of our fellowship. Lean against me and listen to the words, laced with compassion, that I speak over you. You have heard my voice before in the simplicity of a child, in the pages of my Word, and in the inner place where your spirit and mine interact. You have seen visions of my goodness in your life, in the promises set before you, the pure pleasures of your past, and the presence of my living love in the ever present.

Align your heart with my mercy today, and you will not struggle to hear the living words I speak. Worship me with all your heart, surrendering your mind to my thoughts, and you will more easily see from my perspective. Let the beauty of my goodness flood your senses as you focus all of your attention on me. Listen, for I freely speak my revelation-knowledge to light up your understanding.

The starting point for acquiring wisdom is to be consumed with awe as you worship Jehovah-God. To receive the revelation of the Holy One, you must come to the one who has living-understanding.

PROVERBS 9:10

Kindness reveals my nature.

W hen you act toward others with a heart overflowing with compassion, you are living out the very heartbeat of my mercy. When you line your life with kindness, you cannot miss the blessings of my kingdom. Your return will be great when you live a life of generous love.

I tell you the truth: acting in love toward others may sometimes feel like the greatest sacrifice. However, when you train your heart in generosity, you purify your motives. I delight when you reflect my magnanimous love by choosing to extend mercy to others. Self-defense won't get a person very far in life, but look at the rich lives of my beloved ones who live to benefit others. Rather than seeking only to fill their own bellies, they freely give to others in need. Model your life after the generous rather than the stingy, and you will live in the beautiful blessing of a clean conscience. Look to me whenever you need grace to empower your choices. I will always help you!

We will show mercy to the poor and not miss an opportunity to do acts of kindness for others, for these are the true sacrifices that delight God's heart.

HEBREWS 13:16

Holy Spirit is your help.

I have not left you on your own to get through the highs and lows of this life. I built you for connection with me, and you have it. Spirit to spirit, you have access to endless grace to empower you to strength. My Spirit is alive within you, acting on your behalf. Today let the purifying presence of Holy Spirit lead, guide, and strengthen you. I am your very present help, not only working in the world outside of you but inside you as well.

The greater your weakness, the more room for my Spirit to work. I will empower you with my mercy to not only persevere through trials but to also rise up with might. The power of my love is your endless resource of strength in every circumstance. My Spirit within you not only ministers to your heart, but it also rises up within you on your behalf, offering prayers that you could not think to pray. You are covered, every part of your being, with my goodness. I am all around and within you. Let this mystery lead you to press in for more.

In a similar way, the Holy Spirit takes hold of us in our human frailty to empower us in our weakness. …The Holy Spirit rises up within us to super-intercede on our behalf, pleading to God with emotional sighs too deep for words.

ROMANS 8:26

Love without excuse.

I n case you have forgotten, I want to remind you of the lengths to which my love goes. It is unmatched in any earthly container, including the purest loves you have witnessed. There are no requirements to be a recipient of my lavish love. It is an ever-flowing fountain that covers everything in its path. It does not seek to satisfy self but to reach out toward others, for that is the nature of my mercy.

There are no exceptions to the law of love, which requires mercy instead of vengeance, kindness instead of contempt, and compassion instead of judgment. Beloved, do not think that you can excuse your lack of love with righteousness, for righteousness breeds in the light of my mercy. If you truly want to express my heart to others, then love those who ridicule you. Treat them with kindness and respect, choosing to honor them even if they seek to tear you down, and you will be blameless. There is a place for justice, and I will wield it rightly. Trust me.

Love your enemies and continue to treat them well. … For your Father is famous for his kindness to heal even the thankless and cruel.

LUKE 6:35

Join together in unity.

When my beloved ones join together in holy unity, they reflect the uninterrupted union of Father, Son, and Spirit. Surrender your life in loyal love in pursuit of unhindered connection. This love is peace-making, full of forgiveness, and sown in shared joys and sorrows. You are a member of the family of God, a body of believers, unified in the Spirit of your Father. Do not look down on others who do not share your same preferences. Instead, let mercy cover the bonds of community and fellowship.

You reflect my love well when you love others well. Do not isolate yourself or shut others out for fear of rejection. I made you for communion. I created you for relationship with God and with others. So let my love flood your heart and lead you in compassion. Even in this, my strength will cover your weakness. I will empower you to choose to support one another as you lean on my grace. Life is richer in community. Let me show you the strength you have together, lifting each other up in your weakness, extending mercy and kindness in your frailty. In everything, let it reflect the life and freedom you already have in me.

I pray for them all to be joined together as one
even as you and I, Father, are joined together as one.
I pray for them to become one with us
so that the world will recognize that you sent me.

JOHN 17:21

October

I always make a way.

I am the God of the impossible. Some seek my help as a last resort while others run to me as soon as they awake, in the sunshine of day or the darkness of a stormy gale. I freely help all in the same measure, with limitless power, leaving redemption's signature on humanity. I am the God of breakthrough, leading my beloved ones through even the most unworkable situations with miracles of mercy.

I am the One who made a pathway through the sea so that my people could flee the captivity of their oppressors. I am the God of perfect provision who rained down daily bread in the desert. I am the God who led them through their wilderness into the promised land. And I am your God, protecting you, feeding you, and leading you through every deadlock you face. My detours are full of my abundant presence. Just as I led my people with a pillar of fire by night and a cloud during the day, so, too, I lead you into your promised land. Follow me, for I always make a way.

Yahweh is the one who makes a way in the sea,
a pathway in the mighty waters.

ISAIAH 43:16

I am bigger than fear.

Let your heart grow in knowledge of my perfect love in greater measure today. My love drives out fear, leaving no room for the question of whether you will face my wrath, for I am a kind Father, full of mercy toward you. Let the revelation of my pure affection light up your understanding. I am not a demanding Father who waits for you to mess up so that I can punish you. No, when you make mistakes, I cover you with my kindness, gently correcting and instructing you in the ways of my love.

Be free in my loving-kindness. My generous love pursues you at every turn. Let the perfection of my kindness lead you along the path of peace. True love seeks to spread the good news of reconciliation to all who would listen. Let your heart fill to the brim—even to overflowing—with the goodness of my liberating love that sets every captive free from fear and shame. Shout it from the rooftops. Love does not imprison people. Rather, it releases them!

Love never brings fear, for fear is always related to punishment. But love's perfection drives the fear of punishment far from our hearts. Whoever walks constantly afraid of punishment has not reached love's perfection.

1 JOHN 4:18

Don't get sidetracked.

In an age of endless opportunities for distraction, let a single focus guide your life. Keep your eyes fixed on me, the One who called you to life. I will provide for every need, and you will flourish in the radiance of my delight. Let me guide you into my goodness with each step you take. Don't get distracted by the route that others have taken. Don't compare where you are on your journey with those you admire. Their path is their own.

I have called you according to a purpose, and I am working out the details of your destiny as you follow me. Don't stop going the course, for if you persevere, you will find that your breakthrough is coming. Do not despise the detours or the time that it takes to grow your character in love. You can be sure that there are no shortcuts to true and lasting success. You find it along the way as you learn to walk in surrendered love. Your surrender is sowing the seeds of kingdom fruit in your life, and I promise you—it will be sweeter than anything you have tasted before.

Set your gaze on the path before you.
With fixed purpose, looking straight ahead,
ignore life's distractions.
PROVERBS 4:25

Hide yourself in me.

A re you overwhelmed by life? Come, hide yourself in me today. Come with your cares and your burdens, with your lists and your obligations. Lay them down. The weight of responsibility for the world is not yours to bear. You cannot run away from your life, but you can find the strength you need in my presence. You can let me carry the weight of your worries, for I know just what to do.

I surround you now with perfect peace. Rest in the tranquility of my presence. This is a place of restoration and of abundance. Let your heart drink deeply of my limitless love, and you will be refreshed. Find your joy here. Wisdom holds freedom and perspective. Kindness covers you. Goodness leads you. You need never go it alone in this life. You can depend on me, for I am your steady support, constant companion, and powerful Advocate. I will never let you go, and I won't let you down.

Drink deeply of the pleasures of this God.
Experience for yourself the joyous mercies he gives
to all who turn to hide themselves in him.

PSALM 34:8

Holy hope is your bread.

F east on the goodness of my presence with you today, beloved. There is no need to wait to experience the overwhelming, satiating, pure affection of my heart toward you. You are journeying the pathway of peace that leads you to everlasting joy. Nothing can take it from you, and it is no vain hope. Your inheritance lies in the fruit of my kingdom that is eternal. My kingdom is accessible even now as you continue to lay down your life in surrender to my ways.

I don't withhold my presence from my loyal lovers—not ever. Drink deeply of my kindness today and find your soul refreshed once again. Do not hold back from my love, for I never hold back from you. Let it wash over your mind with purity of peace and revive your soul that the world and its worries have wearied. There is plenty here for you, right in this moment. I am near. Take the bread of holy hope and eat it up today.

This hope is not a disappointing fantasy, because we can now experience the endless love of God cascading into our hearts through the Holy Spirit who lives in us!

ROMANS 5:5

Lean on my understanding.

Beloved, there is a wealth of wisdom at your disposal through fellowship with my Spirit. You need never rely on your own limited scope of understanding in any circumstance. Don't ever give up on seeking my ways. I am not a miser with my wisdom, and I am not stingy with my loving-understanding. I will give you my perfect perspective when you ask for it. I will offer you insights into mysteries when you lean into my mercy for support.

Don't pretend to know it all, for the truth is that you are still learning. There's no need to fake your way to understanding when I offer you the discernment of my Spirit. You have keys to my kingdom in the wisdom of my Word. Walk in my ways, humble of heart and teachable in all things. As long as you lean on me and learn from me, you will escape even the troubles of your own making. Walk in submission to my wisdom, and you will never end up in a pit of pride.

Self-confident know-it-alls will prove to be fools.
But when you lean on the wisdom from above,
you will have a way to escape the troubles of your own making.
PROVERBS 28:26

Beauty is being forged.

In the midst of your biggest messes, I am working for your benefit. I am your Redeemer. I restore all that was lost, taking the ashes left from destruction and offering you something new and beautiful in their place. I offer you deep and lasting joy for the tears that sorrow produces. I will never leave you in your place of defeat in what looks like utter failure. No, I am your Advocate, the lifter of your head and the mighty One who miraculously delivers you over and over again. I will never abandon you or let despair cover you.

The kindness of my love drenches you. You cannot escape its power, and you cannot run away from the effects of my marvelous mercy. Where pressure has built to an unbelievable degree—that is where the most valuable gems are created. The greatest treasures are birthed in darkness. Trust me. I will give you gladness for your mourning and turn every disappointing defeat into a springboard of endless hope.

I am sent...to strengthen those
crushed by despair who mourn in Zion—
to give them a beautiful bouquet in the place of ashes,
the oil of bliss instead of tears,
and the mantle of joyous praise
instead of the spirit of heaviness.

ISAIAH 61:2–3

Pure bliss is found in me.

Beloved, follow me into the glory of my goodness. I bless you with my kindness without restraint. There is no downside to my love, no hidden motive behind my mercy. I make it abundantly clear that I will welcome you at all times, in all situations. Run after the purity of my heart like one searching for treasure. You will not be disappointed with what you find.

When you live your life aligned with my ways and in the light of my gracious love, your heart will be full of my joy. There is no room for even a shadow of shame when you surrender your heart wholly to my radiant love. Fix your eyes on me, and you will not swerve to the right or to the left. Your heart stays pure when it remains open to me. You will have more revelation-light shining upon your thoughts than you can write in a thousand memoirs. Open up and let the pure bliss of my presence break like dawn within you.

What bliss you experience when your heart is pure!
For then your eyes will open to see more and more of God.

MATTHEW 5:8

Give me your disappointment.

Beloved, I meet you in the midst of your greatest disappointments as well as your deepest joys. Failure is not a dead end but a turn in the road. Do not give up, though it is okay to grieve what you have lost. I promise that I am still your great Redeemer, making all things new. Even if you struggle to see the benefit of a different way, I will lead you into goodness at every junction. Trust me.

Though the letdowns of life can be crushing, my restoration power will outdo your own plans. Nothing that you worked at will go to waste—not a single thing. Lay down the unmet expectations of your own strategies because I will continue to bring you into a better day. Nothing has destroyed your hopes, even if they feel decimated. Let me show you my higher perspective, where all things are clear as day. I will carry the weight of your disappointment and give you joy in its place. Just you wait.

I said, "I've worked and served for nothing. I have used up all my strength for nothing." Yet my rights I leave in Yahweh's hands, and my just reward is with my God.

ISAIAH 49:4

I have big plans.

Beloved, let me show you what I am up to in your life. What you see as inconvenience is your training ground. When the pressure is on, I am leaning into your heart with my love. I am doing a new thing. It is a new day with fresh mercy raining down on the soil of your life. I will produce what you could never dig up on your own. Soak up my grace, for the fruit of your surrender is breaking ground.

See what I am doing? I am working out the details of your faith as you lean on me. You can depend on me to always come through for you, for I am faithful. What felt like your undoing was the unraveling of false ideas of success and security. The golden thread of my kindness weaves our lives together. Your partnership with my lavish love grafts you into my everlasting kingdom where light never dwindles and life is always abundantly multiplying. Lay down your ideas of what things should have been like, and let me surprise you with my marvelous redemption plans.

Lord, direct me throughout my journey so I can experience
your plans for my life. Reveal the life-paths that are pleasing to you.

PSALM 25:4

Let my heart be your pursuit.

When you set your attention on my affection, you will have everything you need to take you to your destiny. You will find the satisfaction for every single longing of your heart in my perfect presence. If you haven't experienced it yet, it is because you have seen in part and tasted only a portion. I am the same God who raised up a shepherd boy and made him king. Follow after my heart, and I will lead you to your purpose.

When you fix your eyes on me, my goodness will fill you. When you walk in the light of my life, submitting your heart to mine with every step, you'll see that I will always provide whatever you need for wherever I'm calling you. I am your Advocate. I am your promoter. Seek after me with all of your heart, mind, and soul, and I will lead you to where you belong. Let me do it. The road may have some twists and turns, but you will see the fruit of my faithfulness. You will live in the promise of your inheritance as my own.

God raised up David to be king, for God said of him, "I have found in David, son of Jesse, a man who always pursues my heart and will accomplish all that I have destined him to do."

ACTS 13:22

My love is better.

Beloved, my love is more satisfying than the sweetest affection you have ever known. My intentions for you are full of goodness. I am better than your experiences dictate. You will see the glory of my nature as I continue to pour out my lavish love over you all the days of your life. You're never without it. Never without love. Never alone. Never.

I am your constant and faithful companion, and I follow you with my mercy, cleaning up every mess left behind. I go before you in compassion, smoothing out the road in front of you. I cover you in kindness with every step you take. I am not impartial when it comes to you, beloved. You are the apple of my eye; you are my delight. Why live on stale scraps when you could feast on my rich mercy whenever you like? Eat up, and don't restrict yourself, for I never will. The more you take in my love, the more alive you become to the joys of the present. Feast on my loving-kindness, and when you're satisfied, rest in it.

Let everyone give all their praise and thanks to the Lord!
Here's why—he's better than anyone could ever imagine.
Yes, he's always loving and kind, and his faithful love never ends.

PSALM 107:1

I never give up on you.

I am the God of your breakthrough. Child, do not lean on your own understanding. When you come up against challenges that stop you in your tracks, do not turn back. Look to me and know that I am right there with you. I will guide you with wisdom and with strength. I never leave you in a pit of despair—even if you choose to dive into it. I know you better than you think. You do not surprise me, and my love never, ever wavers. Not even for a single second.

I will never give up on you. I am your help, your faithful friend, and your merciful Father forever. You are my chosen child. You cannot avoid the guidance of my grace on your life. I'm never letting go of you. Rest in the shelter of my love, for I will keep you safe. I will pick you up on your darkest days and carry you through the storms that you cannot weather on your own. Let me love you. Open up your heart and you will see that I've been here all along. Surrender your life again and watch as my favor drips from your redemption story.

Love is a safe place of shelter, for it never stops believing the best for others. Love never takes failure as defeat, for it never gives up.

1 CORINTHIANS 13:7

Do not abandon hope.

Take hope today; I have not forgotten you. Though the day may have dawned with heartbreak in your midst, it will end with the joy of belonging. You have found a safe place here—a home to rest in. I won't leave or abandon you today. That's a forever-word. I am still faithful. I am fighting for you in ways you still cannot see.

Today there is fullness of hope in me and my Word. Don't fight the mystery. Let it be what it is for now. You don't have to push or pull to make anything happen. Trust me. I won't let you miss your moment. It will be as clear as day when it arrives. Let disappointing moments float on the wind. You will always have something to let go of and something to take hold of. Today let go of your mistakes and take hold of my strength. Open your eyes to see where I am already working in your life. Tune your ears to my voice, for I have so much to share—a little with words and a lot with understanding. Take hold of my heart as you fill up on fresh hope once again.

Now we are part of his house if we continue courageously
to hold firmly to our bold confidence and our victorious hope.
HEBREWS 3:6

Find your security in me.

I am your great and faithful help in every battle you face. Tuck yourself into my side and hide yourself in me. I have got you covered no matter the troubles that arise. I am your firm foundation, so plant your feet on the solid ground of my Word. The blowing wind will not shake you, for I am the anchor for your soul. You are safe in the refuge of my love.

Though much happens around you—seasons change, leaders rise to power while others fall, and great advances in the world widen the gap between wealth and poverty—one thing remains unchanged: the God who was, who is, and who is to come is your great Advocate. No matter the changes that take place over your lifetime, my love is constant and true, and it is stronger than any powers you face in this world. Nations grow stronger, and kingdoms crumble, but I remain the same powerful God of endless mercy. Find your security in me, and you will be unshakeable.

Confidence and strength flood the hearts of the lovers of God who live in awe of him, and their devotion provides their children with a place of shelter and security.

PROVERBS 14:26

This will pass.

Daughter, do not let the many trials of this life discourage you. You already know that you cannot escape the human experience of sorrow and loss. Even Jesus lived through the process of grief and times of testing. Take hope. Every circumstance you face is temporary. I am leading you to a glorious eternal day that will never darken. It is the hope of your salvation.

When you walk through the wilderness of testing, you will find incredible treasures in the midst of undesirable pain. Walk with me, and I will teach you to see every trial through the eyes of my untainted wisdom. You cannot know the goodness that I am sowing in your story as you submit to my love in times of suffering as well as times of celebration. My hands waste nothing. I am working all things together for your good, building you up in redemption's power. Trust me. Your life is a beautiful tapestry woven together with the thread of my mercy.

We view our slight, short-lived troubles in the light of eternity. We see our difficulties as the substance that produces for us an eternal, weighty glory far beyond all comparison.

2 CORINTHIANS 4:17

My presence will keep you tender.

L ean into my nearness as I surround you with the wrap-around presence of my Spirit. I am closer than your very breath. Just as you breathe in the air, so does the oxygen of my Spirit feed the life of your inner spirit. Rest in my love, knowing that there's nothing to prove here. I know you intimately; I know you better than your closest friend knows you.

As you spend time meditating on my Word and letting grace empower you in your weakness, you will find your soul rejuvenated to life. Communion with me will keep your heart tender, for I melt the coldest heart in the radiant warmth of my love. It is not weak to give yourself over to love. In fact, it is the most powerful force at work within this world. Let me care for your heart, protecting and tending to you in every season. You can trust that I will not let any circumstance crush it. I guard you as you submit to me. It is the safest place to be.

I bow down before your divine presence and bring you my deepest worship as I experience your tender love and your living truth.

PSALM 138:2

My fire refines you.

Trust me when you walk through trials that test your resolve. The fires of life purify your character. Those times are precisely when you should press yourself further into my side. Do not run away and try to find a quick way out. Trust me and follow my lead. I will keep you as I guide you along the way out of every storm. I know the path of each gale. Why try to guess about which way you should go when I always know best?

If you will let the times of testing refine your integrity, you will learn to become even more resolute in life and love. You will comprehend what you could not understand before the fire touched you. I will not let you be destroyed. And I promise to be with you every single step. Don't sway from the path of love, that path that will always lead you to peace. You are becoming more like me in love with every choice of trust in the face of the unknown. Do not let fear overtake you. Trust in my steady presence. You will come out of every trial with purer purpose when you let them purify your motives.

In a visitation of the night you inspected my heart and refined my soul in fire until nothing vile was found in me. I've wanted my words and my ways to always agree.

PSALM 17:3

I am stretching your comprehension.

Let me expand the capacity of your understanding as you soak in my lavish love. When you value my insight more than any other, you will find true wisdom is yours for the taking. Follow in my ways, and you will never lack solutions to any problem you face.

Here is a secret that all my loyal lovers know: I hide myself in plain sight for you to find. I do not complicate my law of love by making you decipher impossible riddles. My wisdom is simple and incredibly effective. You will never regret pursuing my knowledge. And once you taste of the goodness of revelation-light, you will crave it more and more. Look to me, and you will find everything you need for life and godliness. As you grow in your understanding of my kingdom principles, the capacity for your comprehension will grow with it. Fellowship with me in all things. Share your cup with me, and I will share mine with you. I will give you more living-understanding with every exchange.

Where can wisdom be found? It is born in the fear of God.
Everyone who follows his ways will never lack his living-understanding.
And the adoration of God will abide throughout eternity!

PSALM 111:10

Store up heavenly treasure.

When you spend your life focused on eternal treasures instead of filling up on whims that don't last, you are practicing a wise pursuit. Though you will experience great joy in this life, it represents only a small glimmer of the glorious reality that awaits you in my kingdom. You already know the way to build this kind of fortune, and if you've forgotten, go back to the Gospels. I have laid out everything you need to know in the model of sacrificial love. Choose mercy, and you are choosing to put your hope in my Word instead of your own desire for justice.

My justice stands forever. Trust me to do what only I can do, and follow in my humble lead by loving those who may never do the same in return. Give without thought of whether you will receive it back again. My love is an ever-flowing fountain. Let it flow freely from your life as it does from mine, and I will continually fill you up. The revelation of your eternal treasure will not disappoint you. More than that, you will find the satisfaction of your purpose in me. And here I am, already yours.

Instead, stockpile heavenly treasures for yourselves that cannot be stolen and will never rust, decay, or lose their value.

MATTHEW 6:20

I am listening.

S peak, daughter, for I am listening. Lay out your thoughts before me, whether they are pleasant or full of confusion. You do not need to recite an eloquent speech or even offer a profound thought. If all you have is a jumble of emotions building up in your chest, I will hear them all the same. I know you, beloved. You don't have to explain yourself. Whatever it is, you can say it to me.

I speak peace to the stormy thoughts that cause your head to spin. I speak calm to the chaos of anxiety in your nervous system. I speak life over your mind, so let the shadows of fear dissipate in the radiance of my love. I am in no rush in this moment. It is just you and I. Take your time, beloved. What do you need today? What would you like from me? What do you want to share that has been stored up in your heart? There is nothing off-limits here. I am listening. I am not going anywhere.

You will answer me, God; I know you always will,
like you always do as you listen with love to my every prayer.

PSALM 17:6

My Word is stronger than tradition.

My living Word holds life-giving wisdom. Do not get side-tracked by the rules and regulations of religion. Certain boundaries can act in your favor, but empty rituals can cause bondage instead of freedom. Let love be the law you live by, and you will find that I am there with you every step.

Keep your heart pure by seeking me above all else. Do you long to have an important role? Then humbly serve others with compassion, not seeing yourself as better than any other. This is the way to leadership in my kingdom. The last shall be first and the first last. Do not run toward lights and stages, trampling others in your way. That is a surefire way to prolong your path. Learn to keep your heart open and teachable. Model your life after those who honor me in all they do, even when it means breaking the traditions of others. Follow me on my path of love, for that is the way of true religion that leads to lasting life.

Their worship is nothing more than a charade!
For they continue to insist that their man-made traditions
are equal to the instructions of God.

MARK 7:7

Devotion leads to understanding.

Y ou can trust my heart toward you, beloved. When you bind your life to mine, I will not lead you into slavery but into freedom. If you are a captive, let it be only to love. And it is captivation not confinement. Let your life align with my ways as you devote yourself to me. I will always guide you in kindness, and you will live in the light of my mercy.

If you truly want wisdom, then devote yourself to me. Do what my Word requires. Obey me for your own good and benefit. I will teach you the purity of my purposes as you live out the values of my kingdom. Do what you know to be right and in line with my character. This is not a guessing game, and there is so much mercy for your slipups. Stay humble in my love as I lead you further in revelation-light. Your obedience is not for my own sake but for yours. As you grow in knowledge, you will begin to comprehend the lengths of my love. You will not lack insight for any situation you face, for you will have my proven wisdom as your guide. Devote yourself to me, and you will mature in faith.

How then does a man gain the essence of wisdom?
We cross the threshold of true knowledge
when we live in obedient devotion to God.

PROVERBS 1:7

Joy is a powerful force.

You have tasted of goodness before, but what lies ahead of you is sweeter than anything you've yet known. There is so much joy for you. Let me pierce your heart with the dagger of my Spirit-Word that separates the chaff from the grain. I will take out everything that hinders you. Be still now and let me do what only I can do. Do you trust me?

Beloved, the time has come for the consecration of your mind. Consecrate it to my mercy and my goodness. Wisdom is yours for the taking. Triumph is at your fingertips. Whatever has stood in your way will topple over with the slightest command. Your laughter will blow down the defenses of the enemies that stand against you. There is so much more treasure for you to find, daughter. Join with me and don't be afraid of what lies ahead. I'll be with you every step of the way. Have I failed you yet?

Who could ever wrap their minds around the riches of God,
the depth of his wisdom, and the marvel of his perfect knowledge?
Who could ever explain the wonder of his decisions
or search out the mysterious way he carries out his plans?

ROMANS 11:33

Good company builds you up.

Beloved, you are a product of those with whom you surround yourself. If you want your faith strengthened, keep the company of those with faith stronger than yours. If you want to grow in understanding my kingdom, spend time with those who walk with me. If, instead, you spend your days with those who mock and judge others, you will learn to do the same.

This is a principle to live by. For those with whom you build relationships will influence you for better or worse. Consider how you want to live your life and pursue people who are already living that way. If you want to grow your business, you don't spend time with those who talk a good talk but who do nothing to make it happen. Instead you go to those who put in the work and have results. Your spiritual life is the same. Don't leave your growth to chance. Be in fellowship with those who know me well, who walk the path of love, and who seek me out continually.

If you want to grow in wisdom,
spend time with the wise.
Walk with the wicked
and you'll eventually become just like them.

PROVERBS 13:20

I correct in kindness.

I am your good Father, always available and so very attentive to every move of your heart. Remember that I am for you and that everything I do is for your benefit, never to promote myself. I am not a man with a broken image. I know who I am, and I am confident in love and mercy. Trust me, child. Even when you need discipline, I correct you with kindness.

My fiery love wants only the best for you. I want you to live in the freedom of your true identity as daughter of the living God. Fear is not meant to be your master. Pride is not your ruler. Apathy is not your friend. Do not mistake shame for righteousness. Let me remind you of the fruit of my wisdom as you walk in the light of my mercy. You have room to grow and flourish in my love. Anything that would seek to tamp down the life inside of you is not from me. Remember, I reconcile you; I don't push you away. Like a loving embrace, my Word brings you in close to my heart.

The Father's discipline comes only
from his passionate love and pleasure for you.
Even when it seems like his correction is harsh,
it's still better than any father on earth gives to his child.

PROVERBS 3:12

There's an open line to me.

B eloved, there is never a closed door between us. Jesus tore the veil that once separated humanity from my tangible presence when he sacrificed his life on the cross. After his resurrection, he ascended to his throne at my right hand. Through him, you have free access to my presence at all times. I gave the Holy Spirit to you as a guarantee of your freedom and my love. Let the hope that first captured you rise up once again.

I am the God who hears all your cries. Do not ever stop calling out to me, whether in times of plenty or of famine. I am closer than you know, and I am working on your behalf. Let the joy of my presence alive within you fuel your own love as you live in the confident expectation of my fulfilled promises in your life. I am your Advocate, your friend, and your faithful Redeemer. I will never stop fighting for you. Keep coming back to me over and over again, for I never tire of lavishing my love on you.

> Let this hope burst forth within you,
> releasing a continual joy.
> Don't give up in a time of trouble,
> but commune with God at all times.
>
> ROMANS 12:12

Let my presence be enough.

I call you to a kingdom of abundance. You can find everything you need in me. I give you all the grace you need and the perseverance you require to hold on to hope through the varying seasons of this life. There's no need to worry about provision, for I will always take care of you. Whether you have plenty to share or just enough to get by, be content with your present portion by stirring up gratitude.

I will never, ever leave you in your time of need. I don't take breaks from you, beloved. You are mine, and my grip of grace has a firm hold on your life. Feast on the abundance of my presence that gives you access to my lavish love. Hide yourself in my heart, where my delight dwells. There is more than enough to wash away the defeat of the day. I am your great reward, not a consolation prize. As you experience my goodness in every season of the soul, you will find that my constant love is better than life itself.

Don't be obsessed with money
but live content with what you have,
for you always have God's presence.
For hasn't he promised you,
"I will never leave you alone, never!
And I will not loosen my grip on your life!"

HEBREWS 13:5

I will teach you.

Beloved, let me teach you the ways of my kingdom that will promote your own growth. Open your eyes and see that I am already preparing your fields with harvest in mind. I will not walk away from the work that I started in you. I will not leave you—not ever. Trust me as the foreman of your heart and send away any lesser loves that do not match my standards and likeness. You can trust that I won't let your life go to ruin. I will rebuild what has been lost to disaster. I am not swayed or discouraged. I know exactly what to do when the winds of change come.

You are still learning the signs of your budding heart, but I already know the state of every seed within you. Trust my wisdom, and I will teach you how to tend to the fruit and to the vine. Trust me, and your own intuition will grow. Here in the soil of love, there is every nutrient that your field needs to prosper—even in adversity. Let's tame the wild vines within you. If we prune them, we can increase the fruit that they bear. The yield will triple, and instead of fruit falling wasted to the ground, you can use it. Take my hand, follow my lead, and I will teach you.

The season for singing and pruning the vines has arrived.

Song of Songs 2:12

I lead you in love.

Follow in my footsteps of kindness as I lead you on through the journey of your life. You can trust me to supply everything you need for every season and situation. I am your holy help, your faithful friend and your always-available advisor. Look to me, for I will never lead you astray. Truth and light fill my ways, and I make my motives plain.

Will you trust me to guide you into the unknown? Though you cannot see what is ahead, I see it clearly. There is plenty of opportunity for you to grow and soar in my love. I haven't failed you yet, and I never will. I won't ever stop leading you into my goodness, for there you will find the abundance of everything you need to keep trusting and to keep going. My persistent presence surrounds you day in and day out. With every step you take, my mercy covers you. Don't give up on yourself and don't give up on me. I'm not finished with you yet.

Good leadership is built on love and truth, for kindness and integrity are what keep leaders in their position of trust.

PROVERBS 20:28

Don't settle for less.

Beloved, look into my heart and drink in the wonder of my abundance. I lack nothing. Come and partake of my plentiful peace. Let your mind know the clarity of my wisdom and understanding. Let your heart rest under the heaviness of the oil of my affection. You can find everything you long for within me, child. Don't hesitate to press in for your portion. I will never withhold my goodness from you.

In me, there are no hidden surprises. I have laid out my intentions and purposes clearly before you. Dive into my Word and see how I always work things together for the good and benefit of my beloved ones. I am always working for you. My hands are weaving together redemption in your life. I am always doing something new, even if it looks similar to what I have done before. Do not be fooled into thinking that what is comfortable and familiar equates to that which is godly. Let your heart expand as you stretch outside of your comfort zone. There are too many facets of my character that you'll miss by staying on the sidelines. Are you ready to step out in faith and let me show you the wonders of embracing my innovation and creativity?

You say, "The old ways are better,"
and you refuse to even taste the new that I bring.

LUKE 5:39

November

You are pure as snow.

The cleansing tide of my mercy has purified you. Not a spot or a blemish remains untouched by my refining love. You are alive in the overwhelming compassion of my heart. No shame can keep you covered in the light of my perfect sacrifice. Come out of hiding, beloved. Let me wash away the dust of the world's ways and the lies that the enemy feeds you.

You are like fresh fallen snow—completely pure and bright white. Your own deeds did not bring you to this place. No, it has always been my mercy that claims you. The purifying blood of the Lamb covers you, and you cannot escape the power of your rebirth. Do not live as one who has no purpose, for you are full of my delight that will not fade as the days of your life go on. Live in the freedom of my affection that has broken the chains of sin and death. My power is at work in you, so rise up in it again today.

Yahweh promises you over and over:
"Though your sins stain you like scarlet,
I will whiten them like bright, new-fallen snow!
Even though they are deep red like crimson,
they will be made white like wool!"

ISAIAH 1:18

Be united in peace.

Beloved, let everything you do be from a heart of compassion. When you extend mercy to others instead of judgment, you offer the olive branch of my kindness. I did not create you to go it alone in life. Rather I brought you into a family. Therefore, do not retreat from others. This is the time to dig into real relationship with those who are also seeking after my heart. Unity is a holy, worthy pursuit. Be one with each other, in love, as I am with you.

Consider what divides you from each other. Is it the details that don't matter? If so, then lay down your offenses and opinions in the tide of my love and choose to unite rather than turn against each other. As you work out the strains in your relationships, be sure to keep your heart humble before me. I will help you forgive when you cannot do it on your own. I will heal the wounds inflicted by others. When you repair relationships with humility and peace, you are reflecting the restorative power of my love. You will experience deeper levels of my compassion as you practice the mercy-kindness of my kingdom.

Repair whatever is broken among you, as your hearts are being knit together in perfect unity. Live continually in peace, and God, the source of love and peace, will mingle with you.

2 CORINTHIANS 13:11

I honor your courage.

In the face of defeat, do not give in to despair. I will not let you be humiliated. Take courage, beloved, I am your steady arm of support. I am your constant help. When your heart quakes within you, turn your attention to me. I am right here. Weave your hope into my powerful and present mercy-love. In the waiting, don't let anguish set in and torment your heart. I have overcome your fears already with my perfect peace. Receive it over and over again until you are swimming in its calm waters.

I will honor every movement of bravery in your heart as you rise up in the strength of my grace that empowers you to anticipate my goodness even in moments of strife. I will not let you down, and I have not left your side. As you face your troubles, I am with you. Watch as I work out my powerful mercy in the details of your life. Let your confidence grow as you refuse to give fear's tactics a second thought. You are with me, and I am always victorious. I will always come through for you as you put your hope in me.

Here's what I've learned through it all:
Don't give up; don't be impatient;
be entwined as one with the Lord.
Be brave and courageous, and never lose hope.
Yes, keep on waiting—for he will never disappoint you!

PSALM 27:14

True success is found in me.

B eloved, align your life with mine, and you will never need to worry about your destination. When you seek my heart, you will find that the true success you have been looking for is in me alone. I lead you along the pathway of peace I have set out for your life. I have designed a path specifically tailored to who you are. Do not compare your road to the paths of others, for you have a unique and special purpose all your own.

Fix your eyes on me, and I will guide you with steady steps and unwavering resolve. I know the right moves at precisely the right time. Trust my goodness, for I am always faithful to fulfill my promises. I will give you all the courage you need as you fix your faith on my unchanging character. Take hold of my strength, and you will not buckle under the weight of uncertainty. I have got you with a firm grip of grace, and I am not letting go.

You will find true success when you find me,
for I have insight into wise plans that are designed just for you.
I hold in my hands living-understanding, courage, and strength.

PROVERBS 8:14

I am in control.

I hold you fast in the shelter of my mercy, child. There is no reason to fear the unknown, for there are no mysteries to me. You have everything you need in the fellowship we share through my Spirit. I don't need a second opinion because my Word is the first and the last. No one can rightly argue with my wisdom.

Why do you push yourself so hard? Let me work out the details of your life as you rest in me. Why are you trying to grasp for control when you cannot say to the day "Be night" or instruct a bird to become a bear? I, the Creator, have all the power to both establish and demolish. I tell you the truth, I am the only One who sees everything clearly. I work all things together for the benefit of my beloved ones. Give up your futile attempts to manipulate outcomes. You can only reproduce what you already have experienced, and aren't I better than your limited understanding? Trust me. I am good; I am even better than you've known. Give me the reins to your life, and you will not be disappointed in the end.

Here is what Yahweh, your Kinsman-Redeemer,
who formed you in his womb, has to say:
"I am Yahweh, Creator of all.
I alone stretched out the canvas of the cosmos.
I who shaped the earth needed no one's help."

ISAIAH 44:24

It's time to dance.

The delight of my joyous affection wraps tightly around you. Let your heart awaken in the light of my pure pleasure. Set your feet to dancing. Join in with the rhythm of heavenly joy breaking through your cloudy days with the brightness of my radiant love. I am your great deliverer and the only source of unconstrained mercy. Awaken to the sunshine of my love that rises over you. You are my beloved one, and my kindness is shining upon you.

Consider the goodness of my heart that freely flows over your life. Celebrate the unhindered affection I pour over you in every season. I am the I AM—the One who was, who is, and who is to come. I am with you, never even turning away for a moment. Let my delight of you flood your senses, and when your heart stirs in response to my love, yield to it. There's always a reason to celebrate. Can you find one today? Dance upon every disappointment and find your hope lives on fully in me, not in temporary pleasures.

Break forth with dancing!
Make music and sing God's praises
with the rhythm of drums!

PSALM 149:3

Feast on my goodness.

Taste and eat of the fruit growing in your life. You don't have to wait for spring or for the familiar. There is plenty for you to chew on right here and now in your current season. I haven't stopped moving, and I have not given up on you. My goodness is sown into your life, daughter. Just let me show you.

You have more to offer in the present than you know—so much more than you can recognize. Others long for the blessings I have bestowed upon your life. Taste and see the goodness of your current season. Have you forgotten what rich foods taste like? Why do you long for lighter fare when you have luscious and filling foods right now? Don't be ashamed to dig deep. Don't be afraid to share your plenty with others, even if your plenty looks like a scrap to you. You still haven't seen all that I have in store for you. It's so much better than you yet realize. The fruit of your life is getting sweeter with time. Trust me; you will see the truth of my words.

Lovers of God have a joyful feast of gladness,
but the ungodly see their hopes vanish right before their eyes.

PROVERBS 10:28

I have not forgotten.

Your life is a reflection of my goodness. Can you sense my
peace, which I have planted within you through my Spirit?
I am your good and faithful Father who sees every act of laid-
down love that you choose in life. Not a moment of kindness
goes unnoticed by me. I see your love, beloved. I see the seeds
you have sown in the soil of my mercy. When they sprout and
grow, their fruit will be sweet and satisfying to the taste. Nothing
you do in compassion is wasted.

Continue to let love guide you, for it will never steer you
wrong. You can never outdo me in loving-kindness though I
would love for you to try. It will be the worthiest pursuit you
could ever run after. Do not be discouraged by those who do
not appreciate the kindness you have shown them. The nature of
my love has nothing to do with whether it will receive anything
in return. But, beloved, be encouraged, for my love never goes
wasted. Even in the toughest environments, it can thrive. I see
you. Can you let that be enough for now?

God, the Faithful One, is not unfair. How can he forget the work you
have done for him? He remembers the love you demonstrate as you
continually serve his beloved ones for the glory of his name.

HEBREWS 6:10

Line your heart with gratitude.

When you stir up thankfulness in your heart for the present good that is there, you teach your heart to spot my kindness in every situation. Practice gratitude, and you will find that it increases your capacity for delight in the mundane. There is not a season of your life where my goodness is not present in some form. Seek it out, and it will remind you that I am there in the midst of your hardest days. I am with you through it all.

Do not wait for tomorrow to begin celebrating what is here and now. Though some days the practice of gratitude will feel like looking for treasure in darkness, other times it will be as easy as appreciating the warm sunlight on your face. This is not a practice of perfection but of learning to lean into my present grace. Your heart will remain soft in my love as you build your capacity for appreciation. Do not miss out on this kingdom principle. It will change the landscape of your love.

In the midst of everything be always giving thanks,
for this is God's perfect plan for you in Christ Jesus.

1 THESSALONIANS 5:18

My patience does not run out.

In a world that values efficiency over kindness, let your heart mold to my kingdom values. I am patient in love, never pushing my beloved ones away or forcing their hand in any decision. You do not need to be perfect to receive love. In fact, perfection is not a requirement for anything in my kingdom. I empower the weak and make them strong. I listen to the lowly, and I lift them up. Do you want to see where I am working the most? I dwell with those who have humble hearts.

I am tolerant of the inevitable mistakes of my beloved ones, covering them with my mercy and meeting them with kindness at every juncture. In the same way, offer to others the benefit of my long-lasting compassion that does not push or pull. My love is like a flood that covers all in its path with the same capacity. Do not be stingy with kindness or impatient with those who disappoint you. Let love cover the space between your expectation and others' actions. And when you have nothing to give, come to me. I will fill you with all you need to overflow and extend to others.

You're kind and tenderhearted to those who don't deserve it
and very patient with people who fail you.
Your love is like a flooding river overflowing its banks with kindness.

PSALM 145:8

Find your solace in me.

I am your shelter, beloved. I am your place of restoration. Don't hesitate to come into my presence with all the sorrows of your heart and the weariness of the world that weigh you down. I will lift every overbearing thought and replace it with my comfort. My mercy fully supports you. I won't lead you down a path of distress that darkens your days. But when dark days come, I will wrap you up in light and carry you through.

I am the God of your great hope, and I continue working out my goodness in your life. For every dead-end you face, I am the God of your breakthrough. Nothing is impossible with me. Just look to see where my tender love is in your life, and you will see that I am not finished with you yet. And even if you cannot see the goodness right now, lean into my powerful presence. My resurrection power lives in you, rebuilding and restoring all that was lost. You are firmly planted on the foundation of my faithfulness, and I will not let you down.

I, yes I, am the one who comforts you.
All the sons of men will be cut down and fade like grass.
Why then would you be afraid of a mere human being?

ISAIAH 51:12

Align your thoughts with mine.

Beloved, my ways are higher than your ways. So are my thoughts above yours. I see the bigger picture while not missing a single detail. You see in part. Do not give in to the fear-based lies that all hope is lost. I am the God of resurrection and of restoration. I never let anything go to waste. Instead of worrying about what you cannot control, look to me and find your peace.

Align your thoughts with mine as you meditate on my living Word. I am peace-giver. I am miracle-maker. I make a way where you could see no possibility for escape. I cover you with the steadfast kindness of my presence. Do not fear when you hear rumors of rising problems in the world. Focus on the goodness that is also at work. There is no situation where my love is not already present, whether it's in the kindness of strangers or the camaraderie of family. I am always with you. I am always sowing the thread of my redemptive mercy through the fabric of your life, just as I do with every one of my loyal lovers. Fill your heart with hope as you look for my present kindness like you would hidden treasure.

My thoughts *about mercy* are not like your thoughts,
and my ways are different from yours.

Isaiah 55:8

I will do it again.

Beloved, look back to when I moved in marvelous ways in and around you. Do you remember the joy you experienced when I brought you into the freedom of my love? I will never stop working on your behalf and turning your darkest days into beautiful testimonies of my redemption. Do not despair when you face unexpected turns and obstacles on the road of life. I am your faithful guide, and I will lead you with my strong hand.

When roadblocks stop you in your tracks, look to me. I always know the way through and out. Some paths break off the main road, but you must look to me to see them. I will never leave you behind. My patience is long, so you don't have to worry about the pressure of a timer running down. When impossibilities come up, instead of being fearful, get excited. For my power moves in great ways during these times. I am the God of miracles, and I will always continue breaking through for you!

Display your strength, God, and we'll be strong!
For your miracles have made us who we are.
Lord, do it again,
and parade from your temple your mighty power.

PSALM 68:28–29

Don't hold back your questions.

I honor every turn of your heart toward me, beloved. You don't have to worry about asking me the wrong thing, for I want your honest heart, including all of your questions. I may not answer every one at the time of your asking, but I will speak directly to you with the wisdom of my living Word. I will surround you with peace, and you will discover what you are looking for if you will keep on seeking.

Let me put your fears to rest as you trust me with every part of you. Keep knocking on the door of my heart. I will open it with all the loving understanding you need. There is no query too small that it is insignificant to me. There is no problem too big that I cannot solve it. You will discover more than you can imagine when you press into the depths of my revelation-knowledge. Keep asking, keep looking, and keep coming back over and over again. I will never turn you away.

Ask, and the gift is yours. Seek, and you'll discover.
Knock, and the door will be opened for you.

MATTHEW 7:7

Set your gaze on me.

Look to me today and remember that my powerful love covers you at all times. You are not on your own, left to fight a losing battle. You belong to a kingdom that overcomes, for its King is called the victorious One. You are child of the one true living God. Do not forget whose you are. Let your heart grow strong in faith as you meditate on the miracle-working power of your good Father.

Search for me, beloved, and you will not have to look very far. I am with you, strengthening you with my Spirit-life. Lean on my understanding, and trust my Word even when you can't see the purpose. Submit to my ways at all times, and you will eat the fruit of my goodness and protection. It is your choice, child. You will grow in the knowledge of my living-understanding as you practice what I teach. You do not have to see the whole picture to follow my leading. Only know that I see it all, and I am leading you into love with every step.

The Lord looks down in love, bending over heaven's balcony.
God looks over all of Adam's sons and daughters,
looking to see if there are any who are wise with insight—
any who search for him, wanting to please him.

PSALM 53:2

Surrender is sacred.

The most noble and holy pursuit you could ever choose is to fully surrender to my Spirit. There is no greater goal, no higher objective. When you yield your life to mine, I offer you the fullness of my heart and of my kingdom. I guard you with my protection, satisfying every need that arises. I offer you the abundance of my mercy and the greatness of my grace to empower you in every season of the soul.

There is no greater law than the law of my perfect love. Align yourself with it, and you cannot fail. Feast on my new mercies every morning. They will supply you with all you need. Turn to me in every moment and you will find that I'm never busy or distracted. You have my full attention, so will you give me yours? Let your love mirror my own, and the fruit of it will grow in abundance from your life. Nothing else will satisfy you the way my loyal love does. I am pouring it out even now. Drink up, beloved, and then drink some more.

When you live a life of abandoned love,
surrendered before the awe of God,
here's what you'll experience:
Abundant life. Continual protection.
And complete satisfaction!

PROVERBS 19:23

Be persistent in prayer.

Beloved, there's an open line of communication between us at all times. There is uninterrupted communion between my Spirit and yours, for you are mine. I have called and chosen you. When you aligned your life with mine, you submitted your heart to my love. Let every defense that has built up come crashing down in the tidal wave of my affection again today.

Don't give up hope, beloved. Keep praying; keep asking for insight. Be persistent in your prayers, never surrendering your hope to any circumstance you face. I am the way, the truth, and the life. You already know that you can find everything you need in me. When you come to the Father of fulfillment, I will not turn you away empty-handed. Be tenacious in love, determined never to give up. You are already on the path to uninhibited joy where all of my promises are satisfied. In the meantime, press in like your life depends on it, and your hope will be refueled every time.

Every persistent person will get what he asks for. Every persistent seeker will discover what he needs. And everyone who knocks persistently will one day find an open door.

LUKE 11:9–10

Stir up a grateful heart.

Let praise be on your lips today as you remember my faithfulness to you. When you recognize my goodness that is already at work, your faith will rise, and thankfulness will fill your heart. It is good to stir up remembrance, for with it, you will find that the stamp of my loyal love marks your life.

Your present story contains goodness even if it sometimes goes overlooked. Where do you see the mark of my kindness at work? It is surely there, for you are hidden in my mercy, and I will never leave you without the Spirit producing fruit in your life. If you are having trouble seeing the deposits of my goodness in your life, look to me. I will share my perspective with you. Offer your heart to me once again, and I will fill you with the glory of my revelation-knowledge. Keep thanksgiving ready on your lips as you realize the wonders to which I have called you. You belong to an everlasting kingdom that reigns with the power of unending mercy. Rejoice, for you are a child of the living King.

Since we are receiving our rights to an unshakeable kingdom we should be extremely thankful and offer God the purest worship that delights his heart as we lay down our lives in absolute surrender, filled with awe.

HEBREWS 12:28

You cannot lose me.

I am the God who goes after the one every time. You cannot escape my watchful gaze, beloved, and there is nowhere you could go where my love could not reach you. Even when you wander and lose your own way for a while, you cannot lose me. I am with you. You are never alone. My mercy finds you every moment of every day, no matter the circumstances you find yourself in. My love does not meter out in greater measure on your good days. No, it is always an overflowing fountain covering your comings and your goings. You are drenched in my marvelous mercy.

Are you feeling alone and discouraged? I am here, child. Let me wrap you in my present, perfect peace. I have not left you alone to fight your own battles. I am your Advocate, your Defender, and your deliverer—and I always will be. I am a merciful and loving Father, so don't believe anyone who tells you that you can wander outside of my kindness. Turn to me today, and you will see that I am closer than you thought.

There once was a shepherd with a hundred lambs, but one of his lambs wandered away and was lost. So the shepherd left the ninety-nine lambs...He didn't stop until he finally found it.

LUKE 15:4–5

I have set you in family.

Beloved, come close and hear the words that are dripping like honey from my mouth to your heart. Remember that my love is big, and my mercy is all inclusive. You have been adopted into a family of loyal lovers of God. You have been welcomed in with open arms of kindness, and you always will be. You do not exist to get by on your own, and you should not hoard your love, doling it out to a select few.

When you welcome others in my name and tenderly devote your compassion to the sons and daughters of God, you reflect my magnanimous nature. Give honor to each one as fellow seekers of the truth. Offer respect to all who call on my name, simply because they are mine. There is no competition in my love, no need to cut others down to boost your own pride. If you will outdo each other in anything, let it be in how you show uninhibited love. Practice mercy with patience, and you will have nothing to defend if someone throws accusations your way. Choose the path of loving with abandon at every opportunity, for that is the way of my kingdom. Be united in peace, as far as it concerns you, and extend kindness in place of judgment every chance you get.

Be devoted to tenderly loving your fellow believers as members of one family. Try to outdo yourselves in respect and honor of one another.

ROMANS 12:10

Run in my ways.

I call you to a life of holy habitation in which you bask in the knowledge that my Spirit lives within you. When you run after my ways, you are already agreeing with the life planted inside of you. You will taste the fruit of my Spirit when you keep your steps in line with love, hope, faithfulness, and tender humility. As you chase after holiness, you are being purified in character. As you practice my justice, leaning on my wisdom instead of your own, your will molds to my own.

Do not look to the right or to the left to see how others at your stage of life are spending their time. Let my heart be your pursuit, and it will never steer you wrong. I am building a beautiful life out of the continual surrendering of your heart to my own. The foundation of your faith is strong. There is no reason to go looking for better footing, for you will not find it anywhere else. Fix your faith on my faithfulness, and I will work out the details.

Run from all these errors. Instead, chase after true holiness, justice, faithfulness, love, hope, and tender humility.

1 TIMOTHY 6:11

Rise up and follow me.

I am your very present comfort. I am wrapping around you with the overflowing love of my presence, even now. Let me lift the heaviness of these sorrows you have been wearing around your neck. You don't need to carry their burden today. I will give you the robe of my mercy to put on in their place. Today is a day of revelation, where I show you truths long hidden from your comprehension. I am leading you into a new day of wisdom-learning as you follow my ways.

There is no need to stay where you've been stuck any longer. I am leading you into your breakthrough. Leave behind your failed prospects in love and life, and follow me into a new hope. There is so much more ahead of you; joy and freedom fill your future. Your desires are not falling on deaf ears, for I know what your heart longs for. Trust me when I say I am making a way to the promised land where your longings are fulfilled. Though the road of life isn't easy, I am with you. My Word will prove faithful. Take my hand, and let me lead you from sorrow to joy, from death to life, and from disappointment to celebration. Rise up and follow me.

You lead me with your secret wisdom.
And following you brings me into your brightness and glory!
PSALM 73:24

I see your service.

What a beautiful act of worship you offer me as you serve those around you with a heart of love. Even when others do not see what you do for them, I see. I see it all. Though many talk about what they will do, you just do it. You don't spend time dreaming about alternatives. Instead you see what needs to be accomplished, and you put your hands to work and get it done.

Don't worry; your service does not go unnoticed. I am so very proud of your servant heart that lays itself down in love time and time again. You don't do it for accolades, and you don't do it for recognition. Even so, I honor your service, and I will reward every act of kindness. I keep record of them all. Keep living for my audience, knowing that I am so very pleased and proud of you. You are great in my kingdom. Your acts of kindness are widely known in the heavens. What a delight you are!

The greatest one among you will live as the one who is called to serve others, because the greatest honor and authority is reserved for the one with the heart of a servant.

MATTHEW 20:26–27

Come to my river.

C ome today to my river of grace. It is a rushing river, over-flowing and flooding all in its path. Let it sweep over you, washing away the grime of the world. Let it flow over your mind, washing away the dirt of shame and the shadows of sin. You are clean and purified in me. Let the refreshing waters of grace remind you of your glorious freedom in me.

Your heart is my treasure. Therefore let it be filled with the empowering delight of my affection. Let go of the dregs of your limited ideas of success and find your true purpose in me. Notice that as you continually yield your heart, it fills with faith, fueled by joy. You will come alive in my love over and over again as my Spirit ministers healing, washes over the screen of your mind with the purity of my kindness, and fills you with the strength of my limitless mercy. My power leaves nothing untouched when you surrender your life to my gracious tide of love.

I was flooded with such incredible grace, like a river overflowing its banks, until I was full of faith and love for Jesus, the Anointed One!

1 TIMOTHY 1:14

Give thanks in all things.

L et thanksgiving rise up in your heart as you consider all the unhindered connection you have to my lavish and loyal love. You could never outrun my mercy, and you could not talk me out of my kindness. I am your good and faithful friend. The power of my love changes you from the inside out. Look at your life—is there not goodness in it? Can you not spot my kindness there?

When you learn to look for the good, even in suffering and hard times, you are sharpening your ability to find where I am already at work in your life. Take hope as you consider the compassion of my patience. I am not waiting on you to get your life together before I jump in and help. I am your help. I am your Savior. Lean on me and depend on me. I am your support. I am here. I am pouring out my lavish love over you right now, and I'm not holding back. Soak in the delight of my heart and let joy rise within yours.

Let everyone thank God, for he is good, and he is easy to please!
His tender love for us continues on forever!

PSALM 136:1

Feast on fellowship.

Beloved, whether you have a large, loving family to cele-brate with or you are feeling lonely today, remember that you are not alone. You are my child, and as such, you are a part of a big, beautiful family. You have multitudes of brothers and sisters, fathers and mothers. You are not alone, nor were you ever meant to function that way. Feast on the fellowship of your kingdom family. I am with you.

Do not stay isolated and hidden when you can open your heart to others in vulnerability. Weakness is an opportunity for strength in my kingdom, remember? There is a community of my beloved ones waiting for you to join them. You are blessed when you find faithful friends. Do not take them for granted, but with thanksgiving, meet together for the encouragement of your souls. You will sharpen each other's courage and hope. You will keep each other accountable in truth. You will support one another in love, mirroring my nature. Let your fellowship be sweet and true, just as you are. Practice mercy and forgiveness when others sow hurts. Be gracious and kind, and do not give up the camaraderie of your kingdom bond.

All the believers were in fellowship as one body,
and they shared with one another whatever they had.

ACTS 2:44

Turn your attention to me.

I am the God of your present help. I have everything you need to face every circumstance—every hard conversation, every tension, every business matter, everything. Look to me today and find my wisdom is at hand. I offer insights and solutions to your problems. Turn your attention to me. I am God your Savior, and I am God your Redeemer. Nothing is too far gone that I cannot bring life out of it. Just you watch and see what I will do for you.

Lean on my understanding, and the peace of my presence will be your steady shield. I cover your weakness with the power of my mercy. I lift you out of your pits of despair and give you hope to hold on to. I am your deliverer, wise counsel, and your faithful friend. Why try to figure things out on your own when I am right here, willing and able to help you in ways you cannot even think to ask? Let me take the lead, as you submit every worry and trouble to my capable hands.

Turn your heart to me, face me now,
and be saved wherever you are,
even from the ends of the earth,
for I alone am God, and there is no other.

ISAIAH 45:22

I am your great hope.

Beloved, let my love be your great expectation. Just like Jesus' birth was a fulfillment of many long-held prophecies, so will I fulfill every promise I have ever made. Let the great mystery of God in man draw you to the wonder of living truth today. I am your hope and Redeemer; yes, I am your Savior.

I am the God of marvelous mercy, and I am not finished with my great work in your life. Let your heart take hope in my faithfulness. I will do what you could never imagine doing on your own. Lean on my understanding that supersedes the limits of your humanity. I am your source of strength, the power that resurrects the dead, and the life that breathes hope into barren places. My word is true, and I will be faithful to accomplish all that I have said I would. Take hope in my unwavering love today, and take courage in my lasting kindness. When your faith is rooted in my nature, it will grow and produce the fruit of my Spirit. Remain in me, just as I am in you.

"He will be born in Bethlehem, in the land of Judah," they told him.
"Because the prophecy states:
And you, little Bethlehem,
are not insignificant among the clans of Judah,
for out of you will emerge
the Shepherd-King of my people Israel!"

MATTHEW 2:5–6

Depend on my supernatural strength.

I am the God of your breakthrough, and I am the One who offers power for your weakness. Do not wallow in your frailty, beloved. You are in the precise place where my power thrives. Lean on me, and let me give you courage to face the giants in your life. If David, with a rock and a slingshot, could take down a giant who frightened grown men, you can take down the titans in your own life. It is not your own power that matters here, beloved. Depend on me, and I will always come through for you.

When you let your faith rise up to meet your troubles, fear will not overtake you. Let your heart remain rooted in my powerful presence. Let your hopes rest on my faithfulness. I will not fail you. You are not stirring up strength in your own right. I have given you access to my powerful authority through your relationship with Christ. My Spirit lives in you to empower you for such a time as this. Lean in and press on. I am with you.

God said to me once and for all,
"All the strength and power you need flows from me!"

PSALM 62:11

Look for the goodness.

Search for my goodness, beloved, and you will find it. As you live submitted to my love, I am building for you an unshakeable foundation of faith. You are firmly planted in the mercy of my heart, growing tall in the radiance of my glory-light that shines unimpeded on your life. Even when you walk through the valley of sorrow, you will experience the redemption joy that my love produces. When you look back on the path you have tread, you will see that growing goodness fills it. Even the barren wilderness will become lush gardens of glory.

Right here and now, in the present moment, I am your source of loyal mercy. I am your strength—lean on me. Drink up the purifying love of my presence. As Spirit communes with spirit, I am continually depositing my kindness within you. Walk in the freedom of your inheritance as child of the King of kings. Today and every day, you are living in the light of my goodness. Seek out the evidence of this truth, and you will not be disappointed.

Those living in constant goodness and doing what pleases him, seeking an unfading glory and honor and imperishable virtue, will experience eternal life.

ROMANS 2:7

December

Find the wonder.

Let your heart search for the wonders of my glorious mercy, and you will find it present with you. This is a season of celebration as you consider the mystery of God become flesh. There is so much beauty to discover in the wisdom of my ways. Will you taste and see with the eyes of a child, looking through pure faith?

The wonderful news of my gracious gift is upon you. Let it stir up awe within you again. Let go of the weighty burdens of life and lay them down again in my mercy-tide. Take up hope, and let the eyes of your spirit look for the glory of my fulfilled promises. The blanket of my kindness covers you, and the gifts of my Spirit fill you. This is a time to remember my presence with you and to cultivate your heart's dependence on me in the atmosphere of hope fulfilled and joy multiplied. Let the pure faith of your inner child awaken.

What a beautiful sight to behold—
the precious feet of the messenger
coming over the mountains to announce good news!
He comes to refresh us with wonderful news,
announcing salvation to Zion and saying,
"Your Mighty God reigns!"

ISAIAH 52:7

Look through my lens.

Beloved, look through the lens of my love today and find the shift in perspective that you need. Open your heart to love's light, and you will receive the revelation of my living Word. Let down the defenses of doubt and let wisdom's clear voice ring truth into your innermost being. There is clarity for you in my love today.

Lift your eyes from your temporary experiences and look to the living God who sees all things clearly. I am right here by your side, with living-understanding of which I invite you to partake. I offer you my higher perspective today. Will you dare look up from your microscopic view of life and let me show you the *more* of my kingdom? There is so much I have to share with you. Let go for the moment. Let me in, and I will reveal the mysteries of my ways to you. Are you ready for a different point of view? My perspective is broad and doesn't miss a detail.

The eyes of your spirit allow revelation-light to enter into your being. When your heart is open the light floods in. When your heart is hard and closed, the light cannot penetrate and darkness takes its place.

LUKE 11:34

You will see me.

I have seen every turn of your attention toward me. I have recorded every surrender of your own will to mine, and I have met you every time you cry out to me. I offer you the strength of my Spirit, the power of my love, and the peace of my presence. I withhold nothing from you, for you are my child. I will never hold back my love from you. When you press in for more, more you will find.

In the days where it is hard to hold on, I see your perseverance all the same. I've got my firm grip of grace on your life, and I assure you, you won't be lost. When you reach the end of your days on this earth, it's only the beginning. As you cross into my glorious kingdom, where I reign in radiant, loving light, you will finally see me face-to-face. I cannot wait until you can see me as I am, when all of your hopes will be fulfilled—and even more. You cannot imagine the glory that awaits you. Here you have tasted of my goodness, but there you will feast without struggle. You will see more clearly than you now can. Until then, though, you will experience the goodness of my endless love.

I will show my love to those who passionately love me.
For they will search and search continually until they find me.
PROVERBS 8:17

I am your peace.

Beloved, you have been reborn into a kingdom of everlasting peace. There is nowhere you could venture where my peace-loving mercy does not meet you. Submit your heart to mine again today and receive from my limitless love that settles every fear. I am with you to the ends of the earth. I am with you in your staying and in your going. I am with you.

Do not give in to worry when unexpected troubles arise. I am your present help and your steady hand of support in every situation. I have all that you need, not only to get through your trials, but also to grow in faith in the midst of them. You can depend on me, I won't let you down. Let the peace that passes understanding guard your heart and mind as you trust me with your deliverance. I will never abandon you. I am your constant companion and your greatest Advocate. You will overcome every obstacle through my constant grace that empowers you. Let your heart be wholly at rest in my loyal love to save and to keep you.

May the God who gives us his peace and wholeness be with you all.
Yes, Lord, so let it be!

ROMANS 15:33

Prepare your heart.

A s you meditate on the Words of the prophetic voice that foretold the coming of Christ, let your heart awaken in wonder of the great mystery of God in man. I am the faithful promise-keeper. I am the age-old miracle-worker. I am the beginning and the end, and I am everything in between. I am Yahweh. I am the God who took on flesh and became a humble servant for mankind—for you. I am the One who broke the chains of sin and death once and for all. I AM.

I am with you. I am Emmanuel. You are wrapped in the living presence of my Spirit-Wind. You are mine, and I am yours. Consider the mystery of my great love. Now you cannot comprehend its pure nature, but you will. As my revelation-light shines on the screen of your mind, you catch clear glimpses of my marvelous mercy. Even now, as you turn your attention to me, you will find your heart full of awe. Let it soak in, beloved. The God of the ages is with you. I am for you. Yield your heart again to me.

A thunderous voice cries out in the wilderness:
"Prepare the way *for* Yahweh's arrival!
Make a highway straight through the desert for our God!"

ISAIAH 40:3

A yielded life is pure worship.

Beloved, your worship is so much more than offering a song of praise. It is more than a dance of joy. It is more than reciting Scripture in the gathering of my people. It is more than tradition. It is a lifestyle. True worship resides in the surrendered hearts of my beloved ones. It is practicing mercy instead of judgment. It is offering kindness in place of apathy. It is thinking of others as much as you think of yourself, and even more.

True relationship births true worship. You have fellowship with me through my Spirit. You are living under the favor of my kingdom as a child of God. As you align your life—your attitudes, your beliefs, and your actions—with my kingdom ways, you are living a life of yielded love. You are living as a fragrant offering of the purest worship. Let the wonder of unhindered connection between Spirit and soul fill your heart. Keep your heart connected to me, and you cannot go wrong.

From here on, worshiping the Father will not be a matter of the right place but with the right heart. For God is a Spirit, and he longs to have sincere worshipers who worship and adore him in the realm of the Spirit and in truth.

JOHN 4:24

Trust the mystery of my timing.

As you walk along the pathway of love during your journey through this life, do not fret about the specific timing of my plans and purposes. Though you can make grand plans, you cannot control the unexpected twists that are bound to arise in your lifetime. Don't worry; I anticipate them all. There is nothing that can catch me by surprise. Hold your plans with a loose grasp, and you will have peace along the way. Trust me with the timing, and you will find that I always fulfill my promises—even in ways that you could never anticipate.

Instead of gripping your ideals with the tight fist of control, open your hands and let me take the reins of your life. While you see in part, I see everything clearly. You will learn, as you grow in my love and mercy, that my timing, though it is not your own, takes into account everything that you cannot see. You will not be disappointed by the way my restorative strength weaves your life together tightly into my mercy. I will not let you down!

> Give God the right to direct your life,
> and as you trust him along the way
> you'll find he pulled it off perfectly!
>
> PSALM 37:5

I am pouring out my blessing.

Y ou are standing in the overflow of my goodness, beloved. You are living in the light of my glory shining over you. Let the joy of my unconditional love flood your heart and mind today. Let it bubble up like a spring inside of you. I surround you with the abundance of my mercy. You cannot escape it. Let your life radiate with the hope to which I have called you.

Come, rest in the perfect peace of my presence as I pour out my delight over you. I, your good Father, fully accept and fully love you. I am your sustenance. So tell me, what do you need more of today? What is it that you are lacking? I have more than enough to fill you to overflowing. Your life is bound to mine in mercy. You will see my goodness in the land of the living as I pour out blessing after blessing. Rejoice, for my favor is upon you.

May God, the inspiration and fountain of hope, fill you to overflowing with uncontainable joy and perfect peace as you trust in him. And may the power of the Holy Spirit continually surround your life with his super-abundance until you radiate with hope!

ROMANS 15:13

Follow my example.

Beloved, you cannot go wrong when you model your life after my own. Though the way of love looks foolish to the world, it is the most satisfying way to live. When you surrender your heart in humble devotion to me, I fill you with everything you need for an abundantly fruitful life. I have given you my Spirit that empowers you to choose better for yourself than you could in your own strength.

Align yourself with my marvelous mercy, extending kindness to those who offer you nothing in return. Let your heart be full of submission to my glorious grace that offers strength for weakness. I am the healing you long for, the vision that keeps you going, and the unspeakable joy that rises up within you. Find everything you need in me, the source of all life and goodness. Follow me, and I will lead you into life everlasting. My kingdom will invade your world as you invite me over and over again to be your guide and your help.

He existed in the form of God, yet he gave no thought to seizing equality with God as his supreme prize. ... He humbled himself and became vulnerable, choosing to be revealed as a man and was obedient.

PHILIPPIANS 2:6, 8

Keep your heart open.

My Spirit living in you connects you to my flowing river of love and life. You have unimpeded access to my mercy-tide. It flows over every part of your life. Do yourself a favor and don't let your heart build a wall of defense for self-protection. Do you have disappointments? I can handle them. Do you have doubts? That's okay too. Our communion doesn't require perfection; all it needs is openness and honesty.

There's no need to pray empty words, thinking that their spiritual sound will somehow move my heart. Do you want to know what moves me? It is a true heart. Come to me in whatever state you may be—don't dress yourself up or down for the occasion. I want you just as you are. I don't need pretense. I see through it anyway. Give me your real questions, your hurts, and anything else that you're carrying. All I want is you, daughter. Come me and stay open. You don't need to impress me. I love you as you are, and I'm already so very proud of you and the person you are becoming.

> When you pray, there is no need to repeat empty phrases, praying like those who don't know God, for they expect God to hear them because of their many words.
>
> MATTHEW 6:7

Find your value in me.

Beloved, heaven treasures and cherishes you. You are fully and completely found in me. Come alive in my love again. Plant your feet on the foundation of who I say you are. You are lavishly loved, completely cared for, and you are free. Why look for your worth in lesser loves when my mercy fully accepts you? You are pure, beloved. There is no blemish in you.

I will never abandon you. I don't woo you with kindness and then change my character, for I am constant in loyal love. I am consistent in my delight of you. I am the One who created you, so come to me for a fill-up of confidence whenever you need it. I see you in the light of my love. When you start to see yourself in the same way, the freedom and joy of my heart will spread from the inside out. You cannot hide your light. You shine brightly, reflecting the radiance of my glory shining on your life. You are beautiful. You are whole. You are mine.

God doesn't abandon or forget even the small sparrow he has made. ... So you never need to worry, for you are more valuable to God than anything else in this world.

LUKE 12:6–7

Proclaim the joy of my coming.

Let the joy of Christ's coming fill your heart with hope as you consider that what I did, I will do again. I am the God who fulfills my living Word. I am the wonderful One who not only set the stars in their places and put the planets in motion but who also formed you in your mother's womb. I am the mighty God, the One who breathes life into dry bones and raises up the dead.

I am the Prince of Peace, come in flesh and bones and raised to glory to show you the way to the Father. I am the Father of eternity, the only wise God, the source of all life, and the fulfillment of every longing heart. Let your heart fill with the joy of my hope that is alive in you today. There is no better moment to seize all that I have for you. Celebrate with me today as you consider that I am the same God who calls you to life. Behold, your King has come and will come again!

A child has been born for us;
a son has been given to us.
The responsibility of *complete* dominion
will rest on his shoulders, and his name will be:
The Wonderful One!
The Extraordinary Strategist!
The Mighty God!
The Father of Eternity!
The Prince of Peace!

ISAIAH 9:6

My work is not done.

I am with you on this journey of life as you venture into the unknown. I have been with you all along. When you first submitted your life to mine, offering me the reins of your future, you trusted me wholeheartedly to guide you. What do you think now? Surely it is not how you imagined it would be in your youthful innocence, but can you see how I have led you into goodness even if it is different than you expected it to be?

I am your faithful guide, and I am not finished with you yet. You have yet to experience the fullness of my mercy-plans for you. Keep following me as I lead you in peace. My presence is still your sustenance, and it never grows stale. My promises never expire. Let hope rise within you again today with the peace of my faithful love that covers every part of your life. I am connecting all the pieces of your life, and you will be amazed at how they fit together into a beautiful mosaic of purpose. You can trust that I am with you every hour, every moment, working out the details of your life with my redemptive kindness. I won't ever give up.

The one who calls you by name is trustworthy
and will thoroughly complete his work in you.

1 THESSALONIANS 5:24

You are marked by love.

Y ou are wrapped up in the mercy embrace of my lov-ing-kindness. It covers you all the days of your life and even beyond. When you first submitted your life to me, you opened yourself up to the vast healing-tide of my loyal love. There is fresh mercy every morning to fill, restore, and renew you. You are strong in my powerful grace.

Your life is a living reflection of my affection. I cherish and endlessly love you. In me, you will always have all the strength you need to face whatever comes your way. You are never alone, needing to figure out which way to turn. I am leading you by love every step of the way, and my wisdom is yours for the tak-ing. Keep opening up to me, and you will continue to grow strong in faith as my Spirit empowers you. My strong mercy carries you through every season of the soul.

I am contending for you that your hearts will be wrapped in the comfort of heaven and woven together into love's fabric. This will give you access to all the riches of God as you experience the revelation of God's great mystery—Christ.

COLOSSIANS 2:2

Set your intentions on me.

Beloved, look to me today and find everything you need. I am the source of all peace, love, and joy. Do not ever weary of coming to me, for I never tire of you. I hear every cry of your heart—every spoken and unspoken request. Set your attention on me, and you will find that your hope is restored as you remember who I am and what I am capable of. I am the master restorer; I am Redeemer and resurrection life.

What do you need today? Bring it to me. What are your thoughts consumed with these days? Let me into them. Set your heart continually on me, and I will overwhelm you with my loyal love. I will break through your swirling anxious thoughts with the peace of my presence. I sustain your life with my mercy, and I will never let you fall beyond my grip of grace. You are firmly rooted in the soil of my powerful love. Give me your attention, and what you find will not disappoint you.

Every evening I will explain my need to him.
Every morning I will move my soul toward him.
Every waking hour I will worship only him,
and he will hear and respond to my cry.

PSALM 55:17

You are treasured.

Come alive in my love again today, beloved. I have so much joy in my heart for you. The delight you bring me, simply for being you, is unmatched. Though many sing love songs, only in me will you find the perfect love you seek. My affection is lasting, not changing with shifting seasons or moods. I am constant in loving-kindness. You are my chosen beloved, and you will always be my choice.

Let go of the disappointment of unmet expectations in love. Lay down your burdens before me. As you choose to yield to my heart, you will always find an overflow of pure living waters of mercy rushing into your own heart. I will never withhold my affection from you. I do not punish or manipulate you by keeping my kindness from you. That is not how perfect love operates. You are a treasure to be cherished, and your value is even greater than you have been told. I am the authority on this matter, so find your true worth in me. You are so very precious to me, worth more than all the rubies and gold in this world. I never tire of reminding you of your worth, so don't hesitate to ask when you need a refresher.

He is within me—I am his garden of delight.
I have him fully and now he fully has me!

SONG OF SONGS 6:3

Let peace motivate you.

I created you in the image of a powerful and mighty God. You are knit together with love, full of grace and beauty. Your heart is an original work of art, beating in sync with the rhythm of my mercy. Fully submit your life to mine, and you will not be pulled by the ways of this world that call for vengeance and endless arguing. You were not called to chaos but by peace itself.

Walk in the pathway of my peace, choosing laid-down love at every juncture. Your life reflects my own as you offer compassion to those who have nothing to offer you in return. Choose kindness instead of judgment. Be patient in love, choosing mercy instead of retaliation. The peace of my presence will guard and keep you all the days of your life. When pride tests your motives, surrender to the revelation-light of my wisdom. Choose peace over perfection, kindness over self-protection, and hope over despair. You are alive in my love, and I will keep you secure within its depths.

Though many wish to fight and the tide of battle turns against me,
by your power I will be safe and secure;
peace will be my portion.

PSALM 55:18

Let my passion be your inspiration.

Beloved, you are created in the image of love itself. The beat of my heart is loyal love that will never let go and will never give up. Let the passion of my affection fill your heart. Let it fuel your every step. Breathe in my mercy as you tune in to my all-around presence. I am nearer than you know. As you fill up on my kindness, you have everything you need to extend compassion to those around you. You do not give out of a dry well but from a deep and fresh spring of living water.

If you're feeling uninspired in life, look to me. I am the source of all creative flow. If you need a new perspective for a situation where you feel stuck, ask for my own. I won't withhold my wisdom from you when you ask for it. I do not barter; I freely give to all who ask for more of me, no strings attached. You cannot go wrong when you let love be the driving force of all you do. And when you find yourself out of alignment with me, you need only look to me and ask, and I will realign you in perfect peace.

Through his creative inspiration
this Living Expression made all things,
for nothing has existence apart from him!

JOHN 1:3

I have revealed myself to you.

Consider the goodness of these days when you remember the beauty of my first coming. I am your rescuer and the branch of David. I am the Holy One and Messiah. As you meditate on my presence with you as man, consider the surpassing goodness of your life within me. I provided you a way to have unhindered connection with me. There is no need for continual sacrifices when I already supplied the perfect Lamb.

There is even greater goodness coming. There are better days ahead. Though the earth will someday give way, there will be a great revival of hope among the nations as they turn to me. No one can escape the power of my mercy that is on display for all to see through Christ. Celebrate the good news of my coming and look ahead to when I will return. In the meantime, you have all you need in me. Pray as I taught you—that my heavenly kingdom would come, my heavenly will be done on earth, as it is where I dwell. Rejoice, for you partake in the revelation of the Son. It is exceedingly good news.

Don't be afraid. For I have come to bring you good news, the most joyous news the world has ever heard! And it is for everyone everywhere! For today in Bethlehem a rescuer was born for you. He is the Lord Yahweh, the Messiah.

LUKE 2:10–11

Store up my Word.

I speak and dispel the lies of shame that seek to overshadow your purpose. You are free in me, and I have spoken my Words of life over you. Keep a record of my promises and store up the revelation-knowledge that I share with you. Ponder them often in your heart and commune with me about it. I will not turn you away with your questions. You will have understanding and insight when you submit your thoughts to mine, for my wisdom is crystal clear.

My Word is living and active. What I speak is as good as my vow and covenant-mercy. What I say, I follow through on. You can trust that I am truth. I am life. I am the Way. Do not forget to revisit the promises I spoke earlier in your journey when you first learned to hear my voice. You will see that much of what I spoke has already come to pass. This is for your own encouragement and the building of your faith. My Word will always produce the fruit of its seed.

Mary treasured all these things in her heart
and often pondered what they meant.

LUKE 2:19

You were made in creativity's image.

There is no lack of ingenuity in me. I am the Creator of all things. Look around you and see the wonder of artistry at work in the world. Do you lack creative vision? Look to me, and I will give you eyes to see the originality and imagination that already live within you. I did not create you as a carbon copy, so your life should not replicate the details of anyone else's. You are an original—a work of art.

You are a masterpiece, knit together in love. Your cleverness is a reflection of my creativity. Do not despise the way your mind works, for I have given you the mind of Christ. Your unique perspective on the world is a strength and a gift. Don't try to mold your exceptional differences to the world's norm. I created you to shine, and you will shine brightest when you fully embrace your freedom in me. Let your beautiful light radiate from within you as you use your creativity to reflect love's life within you.

Still, Yahweh, you are our Father.
We are like clay and you are our Potter.
Each one of us is the creative, artistic work of your hands.

ISAIAH 64:8

You have my heart.

Y ou are my beloved child, and in me, you have your being. Make your home in my loyal love by settling into my perfect peace. I will never withhold the kindness of my heart from you. There is an abundance of provision in my kingdom, and I give freely to all who seek me. Live as daughter of the King of kings and ask in my name for whatever you need. Do not be shy, for you always have an audience with me.

Darling, I delight in your attention more than you can know. You are the apple of my eye: yes, you are my joy. I have prepared a place for you within my kingdom, reserved specifically for you. No one can take your place in my heart since my love is big enough to hold you as well as multitudes of beloveds. There is no competition in my love. You need not yell to get my attention. You have it whenever you need it. I am everywhere, and yet I am with you here and now. Marvel in the mystery. You have my heart. It is yours. Come and discover the depths of my affection today.

Then the King will turn to those on his right and say, "You have a special place in my Father's heart. Come and experience the full inheritance of the kingdom realm that has been destined for you from before the foundation of the world!"

MATTHEW 25:34

Guard your affections.

Your heart is the place where your affections dwell. It is the place I meet you with my mercy-kindness. It is the place of your yielding and your healing. It is the center that grounds your being. It is good to live with purpose and not aimlessly as if your life does not belong to you. Even in surrender, you are choosing the way you will live.

Do not neglect your inner thoughts or the desires that ruminate in your heart. Submit them to my living love. Let me be the keeper of your heart. Let me hold it; do not give away your identity to lesser loves. There is no need to go looking for wholeness outside of you when you already have it in me. I have connected every part of you with my marvelous mercy. You are not broken. When you live wholeheartedly, you reflect the confidence of your true identity as a child of the living God. Look within today, beloved. What needs tending? I will meet you there.

Above all, guard the affections of your heart,
for they affect all that you are.
Pay attention to the welfare of your innermost being,
for from there flows the wellspring of life.
PROVERBS 4:23

Celebrate Christ.

Let the wonder of my coming as a child for the benefit of humanity wrap around your mind and heart today. I am the God who left his throne in heaven to be born into the sweat and dust of humanity. I came to provide a clear picture of Father, Son, and Spirit. I offered what no one else could—the reconciliation of God and human.

I counted the cost of my sacrifice. Nothing could have stopped the tide of my mercy. Love propelled me, and it still does. I am your Messiah; I am your Redeemer. I am God become flesh, a man who fully lived the human experience. I am God, who forgives all sins and pardons the guilty. In me, you have free and full access to uninterrupted connection with the Father. You are grafted into my heart and into my kingdom. Live in the astounding reality of right relationship with me. I offer you all I am and have. Be found in me, beloved.

Today in Bethlehem a rescuer was born for you. He is the Lord Yahweh, the Messiah. You will recognize him by this miracle sign: You will find a baby wrapped in strips of cloth and lying in a feeding trough!

LUKE 2:11–12

I am Emmanuel.

I am the God of the right here and right now as much as I am the God of the eternal. I am Emmanuel; I am with you. Let your heart dwell in the light of my life-giving love. I do not withhold my presence from you. The loyal love of Christ embraces you. Mercy envelops you. I gather you closely. I surround you with my song of deliverance whenever you find yourself closed in. I am your very present help in time of need. I am your rescuer.

Let the gift of my goodness through my Spirit flood your heart, mind, and soul today. Rest in the knowledge of my living love that breaks the power of shame, of sin, and of death. There is no darkness in me, and there is no hidden motive. I am pure in heart, always overflowing with mercy. I am not confined to your time lines or your expectations. I am so much better than that. Trust me, then let your hopes dwell in my heart as I fill you with my present love.

Listen! A virgin will be pregnant, she will give birth to a Son,
and he will be known as "Emmanuel,"
which means in Hebrew, "God became one of us."

MATTHEW 1:23

I light your path.

When you don't know where to turn, here I am to light your path. I am right by your side. I will give you the revelation you need to light your steps. You always have the support of my arm. No, it is not a case of the blind leading the blind. I see it all, and I will light up your steps so that you can see where you are going. The glory-light of my presence is yours, beloved.

Do not fear when dark days come. Rather, cling to me. Call my name and ask for the revelation-light of my nearness. I will not turn you down. Not ever. I am your faithful guide, and all the days of your life I will continue to be. As you trust my steady hand and the voice that calls out your name, you will see with spirit-eyes from my perspective. I will show you what you need to know right when you need to know it. Trust me; I've got you. Seek the wisdom of my Word, and you will never wonder which way to turn. Rely on me through it all.

God, all at once you turned on a floodlight for me!
You are the revelation-light in my darkness,
and in your brightness I can see the path ahead.

PSALM 18:28

I am coming again.

Take hope today in my faithful promise to return to the earth in final victory. There will come a time when I will arrive again in glorious display for all to see. I will erase the wickedness of evil from this earth and restore all things to their intended glory. I am not slow to act. Rather trust in me and in my perfect timing. In the meantime, know that I have not left you alone.

I have given you the Holy Spirit to help, empower, and bring my kingdom to earth as it is in heaven. Walk in the power of my love that fuels your beating heart. Rely on my strength instead of your own. I am the fullness of wisdom, and I will bring revelation-light to all of your problems as you seek me. I will give you the insight you need. In all things, lean on me and trust my perspective. For you see in part while I see the whole picture. I am coming; I will do it. Live as if you are face-to-face with me already, and you will always be empowered by grace.

Yes, God will make his appearing in his own divine timing, for he is the exalted God, the only powerful One, the King over every king, and the Lord of power!

1 TIMOTHY 6:15

Adventure into my heart.

There is so much more for you to discover in me. You have caught only a glimpse of my glory, and it should cause your heart's hunger for my kingdom to increase as you taste more of my goodness and drink in my delight. There is a deep well of joy for you to drink from. It is never-ending, full of wonderful surprises for you to discover in the depths of my love.

You could spend your whole life searching for a better love than mine, but you would never find it. My kindness is pure, my affection true. Let your primary pursuit be to go after my heart. The flowing fountain of my grace springs up with refreshing water for you and overflows beyond the edges of your life, touching everyone in your path. Let my lavish love be the pool you submerge yourself in every new day. There is always more for you to find. There is a wealth of wisdom and an abundance of bliss. You will never lose yourself in me. Rather you will find the freedom of your identity as child of the King of kings.

What joy overwhelms everyone who keeps the ways of God,
those who seek him as their heart's passion!

PSALM 119:2

Cultivate joy.

Beloved, there is so much joy to discover in the life you are already living. There is no better time to encounter my goodness, and you always have my abundant love pouring over you. Look for me in the details of your day, and you will find my mercy woven into every part of your life. Seek and you will find what you're looking for. Test this theory if you must.

You will find your courage in cultivating the life you dream of right here and now in the mess of things. You don't need to wait for a better time to come along. Right now is all you've got, and it is the perfect place for my powerful mercy to rise up and meet you. This is about digging up the fruits of seeds already sown and feasting on them. There's enough at hand, right here in this season. There is an abundance of growth. It's just under the surface.

As God's loving servants, you live in joyous freedom
from the power of sin. So consider the benefits you now enjoy—
you are brought deeper into the experience of true holiness
that ends with eternal life!

ROMANS 6:22

Seize the time at hand.

Beloved, there is so much opportunity for you right here and now, in the midst of your highs and your lows. I have a perfect plan of redemption that weaves every part of your story together. Seek me, and you will stay true to my heart for you. Align with heaven's purposes for your life as you press into my presence. Rely on me for everything you need, knowing there is so much I will share with you in the details of your day. There is so much treasure to mine.

I will not stop revealing my glorious goodness to you over and over again, every time you look to me. Soak in the radiance of my love. Saturate in the light of my mercy. You are my beloved child, and I am so very pleased with you. Delight yourself in me, and you will be satisfied. Place all your hopes on me. I won't let you down. Though your longings grow, so will your joy. You will never find another love like mine. Make your home in me.

This is where we find his strength and comfort, for he empowers us
to seize what has already been established ahead of time—
an unshakeable hope!

HEBREWS 6:18

A new season is upon you.

I t's time to celebrate the turning of a new page. You are blossoming into a new day, full of hope and joys yet to be discovered. Lay down the disappointments of days gone by, for I will give you fresh eyes to see what is coming. Look with my perspective. There is so much life left for you—abundant life, with sunny days and rich harvests ahead.

Lean into my love now, beloved, and be filled to overflowing with the present goodness of my peace. Let your heart bloom in love's light. It is my delight to lead you in loving-kindness. It is my joy to guide you in my great grace. Let hope stir in your heart even now. Can you feel the rumbling of heaven's dance party? There is so much celebration happening right now. Join in with the dancing delight of my lavish love. This is not the time to hold back your hope—let it burst forth. Let the joy rising within you bubble up until you cannot hold it back. Hold on to my hands as I lead you into the wild dance of your freedom.

I am sent to announce a new season of Yahweh's grace
and a time of God's recompense on his enemies.

ISAIAH 61:2

About the Author

DR. BRIAN SIMMONS is a passionate lover of God. After a dramatic conversion to Christ, Brian knew that God was calling him to go to the unreached people of the world and present the gospel of God's grace to all who would listen. With his wife, Candice, and their three children, he spent eight years in the tropical rain forest of the Darien Province of Panama as a church planter, translator, and consultant. Having been trained in linguistics and Bible translation principles, Brian assisted in the Paya-Kuna New Testament translation project. After his ministry overseas, Brian was instrumental in planting a thriving church in New England (U.S.) and currently travels full time as a speaker and Bible teacher. He is the lead translator of The Passion Translation®.

thePassionTranslation.com